Study Guide

Marriages and Families
Making Choices in a Diverse Society

TENTH EDITION

Mary Ann Lamanna
University of Nebraska, Omaha

Agnes Riedmann
California State University, Stanislaus

D1608296

Prepared by

Carol D. Chenault
Calhoun Community College

WADSWORTH
CENGAGE Learning™

Australia • Brazil • Japan • Korea • Mexico • Singapore • Spain • United Kingdom • United States

ISBN-13: 978-0-495-50793-2
ISBN-10: 0-495-50793-8

Wadsworth
10 Davis Drive
Belmont, CA 94002-3098
USA

Cengage Learning is a leading provider of customized learning solutions with office locations around the globe, including Singapore, the United Kingdom, Australia, Mexico, Brazil, and Japan. Locate your local office at: **international.cengage.com/region**

Cengage Learning products are represented in Canada by Nelson Education, Ltd.

For your course and learning solutions, visit
academic.cengage.com

Purchase any of our products at your local college store or at our preferred online store
www.ichapters.com

Printed in Canada
1 2 3 4 5 6 7 11 10 09 08

Contents

CHAPTER 1

FAMILY COMMITMENTS:
MAKING CHOICES IN A CHANGING SOCIETY

CHAPTER SUMMARY

Defining the term **family** is a challenge in today's society. One definition is that the family is a group of individuals related by blood, marriage or adoption. The family, because of its relatively small size, face-to-face relationships, tendency to involve the whole person, and the intimate relationships between members, is a **primary group**. It is important to be able to define family because so many social resources are distributed based on family membership, on the basis of who is and who is not a member of a family. Several definitions of the family are presented and discussed, including the **nuclear family** and the concepts of household.

People make choices, and there are various **structural constraints** involved with choosing. People must make choices and decisions throughout their life courses. When people are involved in **choosing knowledgeably**, they recognize a variety of alternatives, and assess their options and their preferences. On the other hand, when people simply let things happen to them, the result is an unconscious decision, and they are **choosing by default**. When people choose, their choices and decisions simultaneously are limited by social structure and are causes for change in that structure.

Marriages and families are composed of separate, unique individuals. In all types of families, individuals are given their identity and the circumstances in which their self-concept will develop. Family identities grow and develop and at the same time the family maintains its cultural heritage. All of this occurs with humans making choices. They have creativity and free will: Nothing they think or do is totally "programmed." At the same time, all of the individuals in a particular society share some things. They speak the same language and have some common attitudes about work, education, marriages and families.

Our culture values both **individualistic (self-fulfillment) values** and **familistic values (familism)**. Whether individualism has gone too far and led to an alarming **family decline** is a matter of debate. Even though families fill the important function of providing members a place to belong, finding personal freedom within families is an ongoing, negotiated process. American society does not depend on the extended family to the extent that other cultures do. **Families change**, and because they do, marriages and families are not static. Every time one individual in a relationship changes, the relationship itself changes, the result of partners attempting to find ways to alter their relationship to meet their changing needs.

There are four themes that are developed throughout your textbook: 1) Personal decisions must be made throughout the life course; 2) People are influenced by the society around them; 3) We live in a changing society; and 4) Personal decision making feeds back into society and changes it.

LEARNING OBJECTIVES

Based on your careful and thorough reading of Chapter 1, you should:

1.   be aware that there is no "typical" family; understand the difficulties associated with defining the family; and be familiar with the text's definition of the family.
2.   understand the relationship between individual freedom and social pressures in terms of making decisions.

3. appreciate the distinction between choosing *by default* and choosing *knowledgeably*.

4. understand the importance of family values and the philosophies of *familism* and *individualism*.

5. be familiar with the concepts of *boundaries* and the *archival family function*.

6. be able to respond to the question of whether the family is "declining" or whether it is "changing."

7. be familiar with the four themes that are developed throughout the textbook: 1) Personal decisions must be made throughout the life course; 2) People are influenced by the society around them; 3) We live in a changing society characterized by increased ethnic, economic, and family diversity; and 4) Personal decision making feeds back into society and changes it.

KEY TERMS (page references in parentheses)

choosing by default (10)
choosing knowledgeably (11)
extended family (13)
familistic (communal) values (14)
family (2)
"family change" perspective (14)
"family decline" perspective (14)
individualistic (self-fulfillment values) (13)
nuclear family (3)
primary group (2)
secondary group (2)
self-concept (13)
structural constraints (9)
total fertility rate (7)

COMPLETION (using key terms)

1. Charles Horton Cooley coined the term _____ in describing any group in which there is a close, face-to-face relationship.

2. The _____ family consists of husband, wife, and children in one household.

3. The _____ refers to any group of people residing together.

4. Many households containing grandparents are _____ households, which include other relatives besides parents and children.

5. The economic and social forces that limit personal choices are _____.

6. Cultural change toward excessive individualism is characteristic of the family _____ perspective.

7. An individual's _____ is his or her feeling of worth as a person.

8.	Unconscious decisions are called _____.

9.	The opposite of *choosing by default* is _____.

10.	Family togetherness, stability and loyalty, are examples of family _____.

11.	_____ values emphasize togetherness, stability and loyalty..

12.	The larger kin group is the _____ family.

13.	The _____ family function refers to families creating, storing, preserving, and passing on particular objects, events, or rituals that members consider relevant to their personal identities and to maintaining the family as a unique experiential reality or group.

14.	The text points out that just as family values permeate American society, so do _____ (self-fulfillment) values.

15.	Some family experts do not believe that the family is in decline, but they concur that family _____ has occurred.

16.	Relationships that are more distant and practical are best described as _____ group relationships.

KEY THEORETICAL PERSPECTIVES

Charles Horton Cooley – Primary and secondary groups
C. Wright Mills – Sociological Imagination

INTERNET AND INFOTRAC EXERCISES

Internet Exercises

1.	Sociologist Erving Goffman wrote extensively about the process of *impression management*, including his distinction between "frontstage" and "backstage" behavior. Drawn from his book, **The Presentation of Self in Everyday Life** (1959), a description of the process of impression management in Goffman's own words may be found at http://www.hewett.norfolk.sch.uk/curric/soc/symbol/goffman.htm After you have reviewed this material, give three examples of what Goffman refers to as *faux pas* in interactions with others.

2.	One of the dominant themes in Chapter 1 is the recognition that the modern family is *diverse*. The concept of the *stepfamily* is one illustration of how contemporary family settings are often very different in comparison with "traditional" definitions. http://www.thestepfamilylife.com/ is

	a website that deals exclusively with issues surrounding the modern "stepfamily." After you have explored the contents of this site, answer these questions:
	•	How does today's stepfamily differ from the traditional nuclear family?
	•	Do you think that stepfamilies can be as "close" in comparison with more traditional family configurations? Why or why not?

3.   One of the best-known "variations" on traditional family organization is the *single-parent family*. **Single Parent Central** is a website devoted to the consideration and analysis of issues pertinent to single parents and their family relationships. Go to http://www.singleparentcentral.com. Here, you will find a variety of facts and statistics about single parent families. After you have examined this presentation, summarize in a short essay what you have learned.

4.   How should parents talk to their children about war and terrorism? Go to http://www.familiesonlinemagazine.com/childdevterror.html, where you will find a very interesting and informative article on this topic. After you have read the article, summarize what you have learned in a short essay. Do you agree with the author's sentiments? If you disagree, describe your personal point of view in some detail.

5.   Adoption is an option for many families. Visit http://www.adoptivefamilies.com/ and learn more about adoption. After you have looked at this website, click on the links to the different foreign countries. How are the adoption processes the same in Russia and Guatemala and China? How do adoption processes differ in those countries? What do you think makes foreign adoption so popular in the United States? Do you personally know anyone who has adopted a child from a foreign country?

InfoTrac Exercises

***When you access the InfoTrac opening screen, you may search by "key words" or "limit the current search" by typing in the title of an article that has been suggested.**

1.   The text points out that there is no "typical" family and that a variety of nontraditional family forms are emerging in contemporary society. Examine the diversity of family types using the keywords *family forms*. Read over the selections identified and briefly summarize the different family forms that are discussed.

2.   The text discusses *cohabitation* as one of the nontraditional family forms that has emerged in American society. A related topic is *domestic partnerships*, which includes homosexual unions. In the InfoTrac "Search" box, enter the keyword *unmarried couples*. Browse the articles that are listed and select 2 or 3 that you find particularly interesting. What social controversies are linked to the issues surrounding cohabitation and domestic partnerships? What are your reactions to these controversies?

3.   Throughout the text, the issue of *income inequality* will be involved in many discussions. Using this keyword, browse the articles that are available through InfoTrac and try to find several that relate directly to marriage and family concerns. For example, see if you can locate articles that deal with gender differences in income, or look for articles that focus on the elderly regarding income differences.

4.   The *Issues for Thought* box in this chapter is entitled "Pets as Family." Use the key words *family pets* and browse the articles that are available through InfoTrac on the subject of "pets as family." There are a number of articles that address this issue directly. What are your reactions to the perception of a pet as a member of one's family?

MULTIPLE CHOICE

1. _____   Ernest Burgess and Harvey Locke saw the family as a _____ group.
   a.   secondary
   b.   primary
   c.   reference
   d.   in-

2. _____   The nuclear family model of a husband, wife, and children was the model found most often in the
   a.   1940s.
   b.   1950s.
   c.   1960s.
   d.   1970s.

3. _____   The most common form of multigenerational household is
   a.   unwed mothers living with their families.
   b.   grandparents providing a home for adult children and grandchildren.
   c.   four generations living together.
   d.   parents living with their adult children.

4. _____   The most common household type today is
   a.   married couples with children.
   b.   married couples without children.
   c.   cohabiting couples.
   d.   same-sex couples.

5. _____   According to the text's discussion of cohabitation,
   a.   some cohabitants maintain gay and lesbian domestic partnerships.
   b.   all cohabiting couples are heterosexual.
   c.   since the last census, the number of unmarried couple households has declined.
   d.   most cohabitants are also parents.

6. _____   For the past two decades, the fertility rate in the United States has been around
   a.   3.7.
   b.   3.2.
   c.   3.1.
   d.   2.0.

7. _____   If we try to determine the number of births that women would have over their reproductive lifetimes, if all women at each age had babies at the rate current for each age group, we are calculating the _____ fertility rate.
   a.   crude
   b.   refined
   c.   total
   d.   indirect

8. _____ According to the text's discussion, which of the following is an accurate statement about divorce rates today in the United States?
   a. Divorce rates continue to reach higher and higher levels.
   b. Divorce rates have dropped precipitously.
   c. Divorce rates have reached all-time lows.
   d. Divorce rates have stabilized, although they remain at high levels.

9. _____ According to the text's discussion, which of the following is an accurate statement about remarriage rates today in the United States?
   a. Remarriage rates have been declining for some time.
   b. Remarriage rates have been fluctuating for some time.
   c. Remarriage rates have been increasing for some time.
   d. Remarriage rates have stabilized.

10. _____ Today, a majority of American children live in _____ households.
    a. single-mother
    b. single-father
    c. foster
    d. two-parent

11. _____ _____ family households include other relatives besides parents and children.
    a. Conjugal
    b. Extended
    c. Nuclear
    d. Modified-extended

12. _____ According to the Census Bureau, any group of people residing together is referred to as a(n)
    a. family.
    b. extended family.
    c. household.
    d. nuclear family.

13. _____ As the population of the United States ages, which of the following is true?
    a. The aged will be well cared for because of the large number of offspring.
    b. There will be many more women than men who are married.
    c. This generation will have lower levels of disability.
    d. There will be large numbers living in poverty.

14. _____ Pets are present in _____ percent of American households.
    a. 32
    b. 42
    c. 52
    d. 58

15. _____ In responding to the question "What is a family?" the text points out that
    a. Burgess and Locke's definition is the best answer.
    b. the primary emphasis should be on *households*.
    c. there is no one correct answer.
    d. the primary emphasis is on married couples and children.

16. _____ According to the text, the best way to make decisions about our personal lives is to make them
   a.   by default.
   b.   according to the principles of *familism.*
   c.   according to the principles of *individualism.*
   d.   knowledgeably.

17. _____ *Choosing by default* involves _____ decisions.
   a.   conscious
   b.   unconscious
   c.   sub-conscious
   d.   absurd

18. _____ Placing family well-being over individual interests and preferences is referred to in the text as
   a.   familism.
   b.   modified individualism.
   c.   kinship focusing.
   d.   primokinship.

19. _____ Values that emphasize the needs, goals and identity of the family as a group are
   a.   individualistic.
   b.   hedonistic.
   c.   communal.
   d.   archival.

20. _____ Demographers Suzanne Bianchi and Lynne Casper observe that recent trends suggest a(n) _____ of changes in the family.
   a.   intensification
   b.   quieting
   c.   deterioration
   d.   disappearance

21. _____ Which of the following is NOT one of the themes developed in your textbook?
   a.   Personal decisions must be made throughout the life course.
   b.   People are influenced by the society around them.
   c.   We live in a changing society.
   d.   Personal decision making feeds back into society and damages it.

22. _____ C. Wright Mills wrote in *The Sociological Imagination* that personal troubles are
   a.   private issues limited to individual families.
   b.   a reflection of larger societal influences.
   c.   best understood in the context of the immediate family.
   d.   based on individual choices.

23. _____ The term "primary group" was coined by
   a.   Burgess and Locke.
   b.   C. Wright Mills.
   c.   Robert Merton.
   d.   Charles Horton Cooley.

24. _____ While many of the changes seen in the family are cultural, scholars and policy makers attribute much change in the family to
    a.   a lack of traditional family values.
    b.   changing family norms.
    c.   societal trends.
    d.   economic trends.

25. _____ Which of the following family types would be excluded from Burgess and Locke's view of the family?
    a.   heterosexual
    b.   married
    c.   commuter
    d.   gender-differentiated

26. _____ Of the following groups, which is most likely to be living in poverty?
    a.   the elderly
    b.   minorities
    c.   children
    d.   cohabiting couples

27. _____ Which of the following is NOT one of the different family forms that is seen in increasing numbers today?
    a.   single parent
    b.   three generation families
    c.   married couples with children
    d.   cohabiting heterosexual couples

28. _____ Among American families today, the most common pattern regarding childbearing is to
    a.   have children in their twenties.
    b.   have children in their teens and marry later.
    c.   delay childbearing.
    d.   never marry and not have children.

29. _____ In the seventies, college students challenged university restrictions on cohabitation. Since that time, attitudes towards cohabitation have changed to the point that it is considered
    a.   objectionable.
    b.   mainstream.
    c.   unacceptable.
    d.   tolerated under certain circumstances.

30. _____ Social factors can limit individual's options. Which of the following factors is not considered a limitation on one's choices?
    a.   polygamy is not a legal option
    b.   states placing restrictions on racial intermarriage
    c.   same-sex marriages are being contested
    d.   the creation of expanded individuals options

TRUE-FALSE

1. _____ Americans today are both apprehensive and hopeful about marriages and families.

2. _____ Burgess and Locke coined the term *primary group*.

3. _____ The nuclear family model is often called "traditional" and is never called "modern."

4. _____ Over 90 percent of Americans eventually marry.

5. _____ Childlessness has decreased in recent decades.

6. _____ Non-marital childbearing continued to grow in the late 1990s.

7. _____ Single-parent households and childless unions are not families.

8. _____ For the most part, the more a family earns, the less likely it is to have a pet.

9. _____ The text concludes that the best way to make decisions about our personal lives is to make them by default.

10. _____ Today, staying single longer is much more acceptable in American society.

11. _____ All people make choices, even when they are not aware of it.

12. _____ Family boundaries create a zone where members feel uncomfortable and ill-at-ease.

13. _____ An individualistic orientation can lead us to maximize our options and choice.

14. _____ The juxtaposition of familism and individualism creates harmony in society.

15. _____ Individual happiness and family commitment are inevitably in conflict.

SHORT ANSWER

1. Explain why there is no "typical" family.

2.   Outline the major components of the text's definition of *family*.

3.   Explain how family *boundaries* function.

4.   Explain Erving Goffman's concepts of *frontstage* and *backstage* behavior. Give an example of each.

5.   What is the difference between *individualism* and *familism*? Give at least one example of each.

ESSAY

1. Distinguish between what the text refers to as the *nuclear family* and the *postmodern family*. Give an example of each. How have definitions of family changed over time?

2. Explain the relationship between social influences and personal choices. Give an example of how some social factor has influenced your personal decision about an issue that is relevant to marriage and family.

3. What is the difference between *choosing by default* and *choosing knowledgeably*? Based on the text's discussion, give an example of each.

4. Can *pets* be considered "family?" Briefly summarize the text's discussion of the issues involved.

5. Briefly describe each of the four themes that are developed in your textbook.

ANSWERS TO SAMPLE QUESTIONS

Completion (using key terms)

1.	primary group	8.	choosing knowledgeably
2.	nuclear	9.	values
3.	household	10.	Familism
4.	extended family	11.	backstage
5.	boundaries	12.	archival
6.	the family	13.	individualistic
7.	choosing by default	14.	change

Multiple Choice (page references in parentheses)

1.	b (2)	16.	d (11)
2.	c (3)	17.	b (10-11)
3.	d (6)	18.	c (13)
4.	a (3)	19.	c (13)
5.	d (6)	20.	d (14)
6.	c (7)	21.	c (18)
7.	d (7)	22.	b (9)
8.	a (7)	23.	d (3)
9.	d (7)	24.	d (17)
10.	b (15)	25.	c (3)
11.	c (13)	26.	c (3)
12.	a (2)	27.	c (7)
13.	c (4)	28	b (9)
14.	d (4)	29	c (13)
15.	c (3)	30.	d (10)

True-False (page references in parentheses)

1.	T (2)
2.	F (3)
3.	F (4)
4.	T (5)
5.	F (6)
6.	F (7)
7.	F (9)
8.	F (12)
9.	F (14)
10.	T (13)
11.	T (13)
12.	F (16)
13.	T (16)
14.	F (17)
15.	F (19)

CHAPTER 2

THEORETICAL PERSPECTIVES ON THE FAMILY

CHAPTER SUMMARY

Different **theoretical perspectives** illuminate or explain various features of families. This should not be surprising. After all, no one theory can explain everything. Instead, theoretical perspectives tend to focus on specific features or aspects of families. **Family ecology, family development, structure-functional, interactionist, exchange, systems, conflict, the feminist** and the **biosocial** perspectives have in common that each attempts to explain *why* families are as they are. The perspectives differ in the specific aspects or features they attempt to explain. When comparing perspectives such as exchange theory and family ecology theory, we should not think that one is correct and the other incorrect. It may be more helpful to observe that the two theories do not attempt to explain the same aspects of family living.

The **family ecology perspective** focuses on how families are affected or influenced by the environments that surround them. A strength of the family ecology perspective is that it sensitizes us to issues that are not addressed in other theories, but an inherent weakness is that this perspective is so inclusive that it includes almost everything and, by doing so, loses some of its explanatory power.

The **family development perspective** concentrates on how families change over time, sensitizing us to important family transitions and challenges. The family life cycle focuses on the typical stages of family life. Its usefulness is somewhat reduced by this theory's assumption that families have a common trajectory or life course. A view of the family as a social institution whose values, norms, and activities are directed toward the performance of certain functions for society and for its members, is the perspective of **structure-functional** theory. This perspective gets much of its explanatory power from conclusions drawn from cross-cultural and historical comparisons, emphasizing the positive things family institutions do for societies and cultures. It has been criticized for overemphasizing the amount of social harmony and shared values while overlooking the amount of conflict in societies and cultures. This perspective has been further criticized for failing to point out that what is functional for one group, subculture, or society might not be so for others.

The **interactionist perspective** concentrates on day-to-day interpersonal communications and relationships between family members. In this perspective family interaction is seen as central to the process whereby partners define themselves as persons and as family members, and whereby shared goals, beliefs, values, and norms develop or emerge. But this theoretical perspective has been criticized for being difficult to test, for having weak research methods, and for overemphasizing people's ability to define social reality.

Exchange theory emphasizes how people use their personal resources to bargain in relationships to maximize their benefits ("How much can I get out of this relationship?") and to minimize their costs ("How much is this relationship going to cost me?"). According to this theory, people use their resources to bargain with others, gain advantage, and minimize being disadvantaged, even in relationships assumed to be immune from this type of "calculation." You may want to use your own intellectual skills to think of the strengths and weaknesses of this theoretical perspective.

Family systems theory views families as a web of relationships enmeshed in the broader web of relationships that is the community or society. In this perspective, both families and societies tend to attain a somewhat stable equilibrium. Change in family system affects not only its equilibrium, but also brings about change in society's equilibrium, and vice versa. The strength of the family system is to alert us to the fact that family and society are part of the web of relationships we recognize as social reality. But this is also its weakness as a theory: this generalization is so broadly and generally true that once its truth has been grasped, it is difficult to know what else can be learned from the perspective.

The **conflict perspective** views conflict as a natural, normal, inevitable part of any social relationship, and as something that may have positive or negative consequences, or both. The strength of conflict theory is its ability to direct our attention to conflict as an important, inevitable part of life for couples, families, and societies. It has been criticized, however, for being too "political," too utopian, and as being more inevitable than it may be. The **feminist perspective** emphasizes the fact that what is in one person's or group's interests are not necessarily the interests of all. This theory points out that what one person or group considers a gain may be considered as a loss by another person or group. According to this perspective, conflict is no one's "fault." Conflict just "is."

The **biosocial perspective**, also termed *sociobiology* or *evolutionary psychology*, is characterized by concepts linking psychosocial factors to physiology, genetics, and evolution. This perspective has its roots in the work of Charles Darwin and in the principle of the survival of the fittest. In the contemporary version of evolutionary theory, it is the survival of one's genes, termed **inclusive fitness**, that is important. Over the past twenty-five years, the biosocial perspective has emerged as a fairly significant theoretical perspective on the family. Some critics worry that the perspective has been used to justify socially organized systems of inequality and oppression.

Social scientists have devised a number of research methods to obtain information about family relationships. Social scientists do this because although we may call upon personal opinion and experience for the beginning of an answer to the questions that interest us, everyone's personal experience can act as a blinder. Furthermore, we have no way to be sure that our experiences are typical. Therefore, **scientific investigation** – with its various methodological techniques – is designed to provide more effective ways of gathering knowledge about the family. The purpose of, **surveys, laboratory observation and experiment, naturalistic observation, clinicians' case studies, longitudinal studies**, and of historical and cross-cultural data is to provide us with more accurate, reliable, and valid knowledge about the family.

LEARNING OBJECTIVES

Based on your careful and thorough reading of Chapter 2, you should:

1.   understand the use of different theoretical perspectives in studying the family.

2.   be familiar with the eight theoretical perspectives discussed in this chapter: family ecology, family development, structure-functional, interactionist, exchange, family systems, feminist, and biosocial.

3.   be familiar with the different family-related customs, practices, and rules in different cultures in the world.

4.   understand how personal experience can act as a "blinder."

5.   understand how scientific investigation can remove blinders.

6.   be familiar with the different frameworks involved with studying ethnic minority families: cultural equivalent, cultural deviant, cultural variant, and kin-scripts.

7.   be familiar with the different research methods discussed in this chapter: surveys, experiments, naturalistic observation, case studies, longitudinal studies, and historical and cross-cultural data.

KEY TERMS (page references in parentheses)

agreement reality (38)
biosocial perspective (36)
boundary ambiguity (34)
case study (41)
conflict perspective (35)
developmental task (27)
emerging adulthood (28)
equilibrium (34)
evolutionary heritage (36)
exchange balance (33)
exchange theory (33)
experiential reality (38)
experiment (40)
extended family (29)
family boundaries (34)
family development perspective (27)
family ecology perspective (22)
family function (30)
family life cycle (27)
family policy (24)
family structure (29)
family systems theory (34)
feminist perspective (35)
identity (31)
inclusive fitness (36)
informed consent (39)
interaction (31)

interactionist perspective (31)
internalize (32)
institutional review board (IRB) (38)
laboratory observation (40)
longitudinal study (41)
looking-glass self (32)
meaning (32)
naturalistic observation (41)
normative order hypothesis (27)
nuclear family (29)
on-time transition (27)
patriarchy (35)
principle of least interest (33)
resources (33)
rewards and costs (33)
role (32)
role-making (32)
role sequencing (27)
role-taking (32)
science (38)
scientific investigation (39)
self-concept (31)
social institution (29)
structure-functional perspective (29)
survey (39)
system (34)
theoretical perspective (22)

COMPLETION (using key terms)

1.   A _____ leads researchers to identify those aspects of families that are of interest to them and suggests explanations for why family patterns and practices are the way they are.

2.   From the _____ perspective, society is viewed as part of families' environment, placing limitations and constraints on families, but also as opening up possibilities and opportunities.

3.   In a narrow sense, _____ is all the procedures, regulations, attitudes, and goals of government that affect families.

4.   The _____ perspective emphasizes that the family itself is a unit of analysis and that the family changes in predictable ways over time.

5.   The _____ perspective has been criticized for overestimating the amount of shared values, cooperation and equilibrium, and overlooking or de-emphasizing the amount of conflict and stress in social institutions and structures.

6.   _____ refers to what a given activity or statement conveys symbolically.

7.   _____ refers to the basic feelings people have about themselves, their abilities, and their worth.

8.   The _____ has been criticized for overestimating the degree to which family members create realities of their own making as compared to the "real" reality in which they find themselves.

9.   _____ theory grew out of the application of an economic perspective to social relationships.

10.   _____ theory uses the model of a system.

11.   Feminist theories derive from the broader _____ perspective.

12.   The biosocial perspective emphasizes _____: It is the survival of one's genes that is important.

13.   In the _____ research method, samples of persons are contacted by telephone, mail, or in person, and are asked to respond to interviews or questionnaires, after which the data are analyzed and conclusions are drawn.

14.   Carefully measured, monitored, and controlled conditions are necessary if family researchers are to use the research method called the _____.

15.   In the research method termed _____, investigators view family behavior as it actually happens in its natural setting.

16.   Scientists conduct _____ when they get information about individuals, families, or larger groups and do so in such a way as to make comparisons over a longer period of time.

KEY THEORETICAL PERSPECTIVES

family ecology
family development
structure-functionalism
interactionism

exchange theory
family systems theory
feminist perspectives
biosocial perspectives

INTERNET AND INFOTRAC EXERCISES

<u>Internet Exercises</u>

1.   Go to: http://www.hewett.norfolk.sch.uk/CURRIC/soc/Theory1.htm. Welcome to **the Sociological Theory**. After you have accessed this site, click on *The Durkheim Page* for a review of functionalism; click on *The Karl Marx Page* for a discussion of the conflict perspective; then click on *Social Interactionism* for a different look at the interactionist perspective. If you have time, you may wish to explore other social theorists who are highlighted within this website. After you have explored the Sociological Theory site, answer the following questions:

- What are the core assumptions of each major theoretical perspective (functionalist, conflict, and interactionist)?
- All of the early social theorists, such as Emile Durkheim, Karl Marx, and Max Weber, had certain concerns in common. What are some of these common concerns and how do they relate to the perceived social problems during the time periods involved?

2.   Go to http://www.hewett.norfolk.sch.uk/CURRIC/soc/postmode/postm.htm to learn about Post-Modern Theory. After you have read the different sections on Modern and Post Modern Theory, how do these perspectives apply to the study of marriage and the family?

3.   Here's a different strategy for understanding the feminist perspective. Take a look at a position paper entitled "The Radical Feminist Perspective in the Field of Sociology": http://home.earthlink.net/~ahunter/RFvLitCrit/tocandtp.html After you have read this paper, answer these questions: 1) Have you ever been in a marginalized position as was the author of this paper? 2) Do you agree with the radical feminist perspective as defined by this author?

4.   Go to http://marriage.rutgers.edu/Publications/SOOU/TEXTSOOU2004.htm   Read Barbara Dafoe and David Popenoe's article on the State of Our Unions: The Social Health of Marriage in America. What are the indicators of marital health and well being? How are they measured. Should there be other indicators?

<u>InfoTrac Exercises</u>

1.   Enter the keywords *paradigm shifts in family sociology*. You will find an article by Susan Mann and her colleagues concerning which theoretical perspective(s) is/are dominant in family sociology today. Read the article and then write a short summary of the content and significance of this article. Which theoretical perspective do you tend to favor? Why?

2.   Enter the keywords *Francis M. Kozub; the family systems theory*. Read Ms. Kozub's article. Write a short position paper on your impressions of this particular perspective. In the paper, make at least one suggestion for a marriage and family-related topic that could be researched using this approach.

3.   The *Issues for Thought* insert deals with the topic of safety and risk in the family environment. Enter the keywords *childhood injuries; issues for the family physician*. Read the article by Glotzer and Weitzman. Compare the contents of this article with the key points that are made in the *Issues* insert. What are the major similarities?

Chapter 2

MULTIPLE CHOICE

1. _____   The purpose of all theoretical perspectives is to
    a.   move from multiple small-scale explanations toward a larger, comprehensive explanation.
    b.   increase our understanding.
    c.   make research methods more reliable and valid.
    d.   become as abstract as possible within the limits of the topic under investigation.

2. _____   How families are affected by their neighborhoods and how neighborhoods affect individual families is part of which perspective?
    a.   family ecology
    b.   structure-functional
    c.   interactionist
    d.   family development

3. _____   Which of the following is consistent with the main concerns of the family ecology theoretical perspective?
    a.   the family as a child-rearing institution
    b.   the conflict feminist perspective
    c.   laboratory observations and longitudinal designs
    d.   development of family policy

4. _____   Which of the following is an important part of the family development theoretical perspective?
    a.   family life cycle
    b.   removing blinders by means of scientific research
    c.   the family as an economic unit
    d.   kin-work and kin-time

5. _____   Patty and Al find that their relationship is changing rapidly due to the arrival of their first child. Their relationships is not necessarily "worse," but it is rapidly becoming more complex and has changed dramatically. Patty and Al are in which stage of the family life cycle?
    a.   second
    b.   third
    c.   fourth
    d.   sixth

6. _____   The family development perspective emerged and had wide acceptance during
    a.   1880-1910.
    b.   1910-1920.
    c.   1930-1950.
    d.   1960-1980.

7. _____ Which of the following characterizes the family development perspective?
   a. It has a white, middle-class bias.
   b. It is similar to the family systems approach.
   c. It is not applicable to the study of large populations.
   d. It is not applicable to families consisting of middle-aged or older partners whose adult children had left home.

8. _____ "The family provides order and predictability to social relationships, a sense of emotional security, and a satisfying feeling of belonging." This statement is linked to which perspective?
   a. family systems
   b. exchange
   c. interactionist
   d. structure-functional

9. _____ Activities such as raising children reasonably, providing economic support, and giving emotional security are the main focus of which theoretical perspective?
   a. interactionist
   b. family development
   c. structure-functional
   d. exchange

10. _____ The modern family is no longer a(n)
   a. mechanism for socialization and/or social control of infants and children.
   b. important source of emotional security and support, with these tasks now being met by peer groups.
   c. location for physical and psychological boundaries.
   d. self-sufficient economic unit.

11. _____ Which of the following theoretical perspectives views people's self concepts and identity as emerging within the family?
   a. developmental
   b. interactionist
   c. structure-functional
   d. feminist

12. _____ Which of the following grew out of the application of an economic perspective to social relationships?
   a. the structure-functional perspective
   b. the interactionist perspective
   c. exchange theory
   d. family development

13. _____ The _____ perspective can show how things fit together and how "everything affects everything else" within the family.
   a. family systems
   b. exchange
   c. developmental
   d. feminist

14. _____ Like the conflict perspective, the feminist perspective
  a. assumes that society is dependent on equilibrium for proper functioning.
  b. calls attention to unequal power within groups and the larger society.
  c. emphasizes exchange.
  d. sees human interactions as the basis for social life.

15. _____ Which perspective presumes that certain human behaviors are both "natural" and difficult to change?
  a. feminist
  b. exchange
  c. biosocial
  d. interactionist

16. _____ According to the text, by definition a system, such as a family, always moves toward
_____.
  a. change
  b. boundaries
  c. equilibrium
  d. ambiguity

17. _____ A research method that frequently makes use of a "random sample" is
  a. the experiment.
  b. survey.
  c. the longitudinal study.
  d. the clinicians' case study.

18. _____ In _____, the researcher lives with a family or social group or spends extensive time with family or group members.
  a. naturalistic observation
  b. surveys
  c. the longitudinal study
  d. the clinicians' case study

19. _____ Which of the following is an unavoidable factor in a longitudinal research study or project, but instead is planned and must occur if the research is longitudinal?
  a. recruitment of a relatively large number of research participants
  b. precise measurement, often accompanied by computer-based data analysis
  c. the passage of time
  d. researchers being non-judgmental about the observed behavior

20. _____ All research tools represent
  a. the main reason for selecting a specific theory to guide the research.
  b. the scientific community to the general public.
  c. a compromise, because each research tool has pros and cons.
  d. the individual research or research team's level of commitment to the research project, because some research tools require more commitment than other such tools.

21. _____ According to the normative order hypothesis, which of the following is best for mental health and happiness?
    a.   parenthood, work, marriage
    b.   work, marriage, parenthood
    c.   marriage, parenthood, divorce
    d.   work, parenthood, marriage

22. _____ Neighborhoods are important in the development of children but have risks as well. Which of the following is NOT one of the risk factors associated with neighborhoods?
    a.   high crime rates
    b.   low educational attainment
    c.   quality day care
    d.   female-headed households

23. _____ Family policy concerns itself with all of the following except:
    a.   goals of the government
    b.   family procedure
    c.   ways in which research is conducted
    d.   regulations regarding family housing

24. _____ We have all grown up in a family and "know" about the family. This is called
    a.   agreement reality.
    b.   first hand experience.
    c.   experiential reality.
    d.   actual knowledge.

25. _____ Historical data is useful for which of the following?
    a.   studies of the causes of family stability
    b.   analysis of the family institution
    c.   guide for observational research
    d.   biosocial events in families

26. _____ Science is a logical system that bases knowledge on
    a.   experiential reality.
    b.   agreement reality.
    c.   empirical evidence.
    d.   casual observation.

27. _____ To assure that research on human subjects adheres to professional and ethical standards, most institutions require review from
    a.   human subject review committee.
    b.   human factors analysis board.
    c.   institutional review board.
    d.   departmental research committee.

28. _____ Research using an experimental design involves two groups. Which of the groups receives the treatment?
   a. control group
   b. experimental group
   c. design groups
   d. laboratory group

29. _____ The advantage of a case study is that it is _____.
   a. subjective
   b. biased
   c. a detailed account of family life
   d. never totally accurate

30. _____ Boundary ambiguity is commonly found in which of the following family types?
   a. extended families
   b. nuclear families
   c. step families
   d. gay and lesbian families

TRUE-FALSE

1. _____ Theoretical perspectives are ways of viewing reality; they are lenses through which observers organize and interpret what they see.

2. _____ The text discusses eight theoretical perspectives, including the family ecology and family development perspectives.

3. _____ The family ecology perspective explores ways in which families are interdependent with their environments.

4. _____ The increasing globalization of the sociocultural environment of families means that job opportunities for American family members are separated from the decisions of multinational corporations.

5. _____ Feminist perspectives about family seem to be most consistent and to conflict very little with the ideas of structure-functional theory.

6. _____ Viewing the family as a social institution with economic, educational, and other important tasks to perform for individual family members, for families, and for society as a whole, is most consistent with the structure-functional theory.

7. _____ Exchange theory grew out of the application of an economic perspective to social relationships.

8. _____ The interactionist perspective is a subcategory of the conflict perspective, focusing on large-scale relationships involving relatively large numbers of people.

9. _____ Family systems theory tends to look at the family as a whole.

10. _____ The central focus of feminist perspectives is on economic issues.

11. _____ The biosocial perspective has its roots in Talcott Parsons' work on society as a social system.

12. _____ A representative sample is one in which every member of the population has an equal chance of being chosen.

13. _____ Surveys are by their very nature an unscientific way to study families.

14. _____ The fact that people who present themselves for counseling may differ in important ways from those who do not is an inherent weakness in the use of clinicians' case studies.

15. _____ Longitudinal studies obtain and analyze information about changes that happen over a considerable length of time: weeks, months, years, decades, or longer.

SHORT ANSWER

1. Distinguish between family development theory and interactionist theory.

2. Compare and contrast the feminist theory with exchange theory. In what ways are they similar and different to each other?

3.   Explain how personal experience can act as "blinders," preventing more complete understanding of couples and families.

4.   Distinguish between longitudinal research and historical data.

5.   Explain the advantages and disadvantages of survey research when studying the family.

ESSAY

1. Of the various theories of family, no one theory is "the correct theory." Explain why.

2. Pick four of the eight theoretical perspectives discussed in the text and explain each one in some detail.

3. Compare and contrast the structure-functional perspective with the feminist perspective.

4. Explore the strengths and weaknesses of each of the methods of social science discussed in the textbook.

5. Each theory discussed in the textbook lends itself to some research methods more than others. Select *one* theoretical perspective and write an essay in which you point out (1) the research methods that seem particularly well-suited to research guided by that theory and (2) the research methods that should probably be avoided in research guided by that theory. You may find it helpful to use an example to be used in illustration as you write your essay.

ANSWERS TO SAMPLE QUESTIONS

Completion (using key terms)

1. theoretical perspective
2. family ecology
3. family policy
4. family development
5. structure-functional
6. Meaning
7. Self-concept
8. interactionist
9. Exchange
10. Family systems
11. conflict
12. inclusive fitness
13. survey
14. experiment
15. naturalistic observation
16. longitudinal studies

Multiple Choice (page references in parentheses)

1. b (22)
2. a (22)
3. d (24)
4. a (27)
5. a (27)
6. c (27)
7. a (27)
8. d (29)
9. c (29)
10. d (31)
11. b (33)
12. c (33)
13 a (34)
14. b (35)
15. c (36)
16. c (34)
17. b (39)
18. a (41)
19. c (41)
20. c (42)
21. b (27)
22. c (26)
23. c (24)
24. c (38)
25. b (42)
26. c (38)
27. c (38)
28. b (40)
29. c (41)
30. c (34)

True-False (page references in parentheses)

1. T (22)
2. T (22)
3. T (22)
4. F (26)
5. F (35)
6. T (29)
7. T (33)
8. F (31)
9. T (34)
10. F (34)
11. F (36)
12. T (39)
13. F (39)
14. T (41)
15. T (41)

CHAPTER 3

AMERICAN FAMILIES IN SOCIAL CONTEXT

CHAPTER SUMMARY

This chapter begins with the observation that individuals and families vary as a result of the social settings in which they exist and that social-historical circumstances impact families in all societies and cultures.

Specific historical events and conditions – war and depression, for example– affect options, choices, and the everyday lives of families. In the Depression years, couples delayed marriage and parenthood and had fewer children than they wanted. During the 1950s, family life was not so overshadowed by national crisis. In the 1960s and 1970s, marriage rates declined and divorce rates increased dramatically. Today, a husband is far less likely to earn a family wage and the twin-income family is the norm. The present historical moment is one of adaptation to profound cultural change and economic ups and downs much affected by **globalization** of the economy.

One of the most dramatic developments of the twentieth century has been the increased longevity and changing age structure of our population. Not only are people living longer, but the elderly now compose a larger proportion of our population. The elderly are an increasing presence in society because families are having fewer children than they did in the past. The increasing numbers of elderly people must be cared for by a smaller group of middle-aged and young adults. The declining proportion of children is likely to affect public policy support for families raising children.

Social class may be as important as race or ethnicity in affecting people's choices and **life chances**. The distribution of income in the United States is highly unequal. Poverty rates fell in the 1960s and have risen and fallen again since then. Money may not buy happiness, but it does afford a myriad of options. Besides distinguishing families on the basis of income and assets, social scientists have often compared white- and blue-collar workers.

Race is a social construction reflecting how Americans think about race; **ethnicity** has no biological connotations, but refers to culture: language, customs, and history. African Americans, Hispanics, American Indians, Asians, and Pacific Islanders are often grouped into a category termed **minority group**. The United States is an increasingly diverse nation: Minorities are now almost one-third of the population. African Americans are increasingly split into a middle class that has benefited from the opportunities opened by the Civil Rights movement and a substantial sector that remains disadvantaged. A higher proportion of black children than in other racial/ethnic groups lives in poverty. Throughout the twentieth century, the percentage of black children with at least one absent parent has been about twice that for whites. The "retreat from marriage" by blacks is not due to differences in beliefs about the value of marriage. As a family system, African American families are child-focused, but are also among the groups more likely to care for aging family members. Latinos (Hispanics) are now the largest minority group in the U.S. There is enormous diversity within the Latino population. There is continuity as well as change for Latinos who come to the U.S. Asian/Pacific Islanders are often termed a "model minority" because of their strong educational attainment, high representation in managerial and professional occupations, and family incomes that are highest of all racial/ethnic groups. Asian/Pacific Islander families are more cohesive and less individualistic than white families. A unique feature of Native American families is the relationship of tribal societies to the U.S. government. **Miller's typology of Native American families** posited a continuum from traditional to transitional to bicultural to marginal families. Whites continue to be the numerical majority in the United States; they are largely of European descent. Much that is written about "the family" is grounded in common patterns among middle-class whites. Non-Hispanic whites have advantages in American society that go unnoticed by them. Multiracial and multiethnic families are created by marriage, by establishment of an unmarried-couple household, and by adoption of children who are of a different race than their new parents.

The historically dominant religion in the U.S. has been Protestantism. The formalities of doctrine have not always had the effect we might assume on family-related behavior. Religion affects family life in complex and sometimes unexpected ways. When we consider family diversity, we usually don't think of regional variation.

Technology has always affected family life. Recently, links between family and technology have taken the form of electronic devices and biomedical breakthroughs. Computer-based technology and handheld devices enable family members to remain in close touch. E-mail supports communication within the extended family. The Internet may help form families. Videoconferencing is a new development in the lives of postdivorce families. Thanks to electronic surveillance, parents may check on children; partners on their spouses and lovers; and families on hired caregivers. Technology has pros and cons, but its most important impact in terms of the family is *change*. Technology can transform family relationships.

LEARNING OBJECTIVES

Based on your careful and thorough reading of Chapter 3, you should:

1. be familiar with the historical events that have shaped options, choices, and the everyday lives of families, including the phenomenon of globalization.

2. understand the implications of the increased longevity of the American population.

3. understand race, ethnicity, and minority groups as social constructions.

4. be familiar with the social characteristics of families among African Americans, Latinos (Hispanics) Asian and Pacific Islanders, American Indians (Native Americans), and whites.

5. be familiar with how religion, region, and rural-urban residence relate to family structure in American society.

6. understand the significance of the economy and social class for families in American society.

7. understand how technology has affected family life, paying special attention to communication and surveillance technology, and to biomedical advances.

KEY TERMS (page references in parentheses)

binational family (60)
cultural deviant perspective (57)
cultural equivalent perspective (57)
cultural variant perspective (57)
ethnicity, ethnic identity (55)
Euro-American families (67)
globalization (51)
infant mortality rate (61)
life chances (49)

Miller's typology of urban Native American
    families (67)
    traditional (67)
    transitional (67)
    bicultural (67)
    marginal (67)
race (54)
segmented assimilation (60)
sex ratio (59)
social class (53)
transnational family (62)
undocumented immigrants (60)

COMPLETION (using key terms)

1. _____ (illegal) immigrants enter the U.S. at a rate of about 275,000 annually.

2. One of the adjustment problems of immigrant families is the _____ that can occur when children learn the English language and American ways faster than their parents.

3. The text points out that _____ is a social construction, reflecting how Americans *think* about this concept.

4. _____ has no biological connotations, but refers to culture: language, customs, and history.

5. _____ conveys the idea that persons in those groups experience some disadvantage, exclusion, or discrimination in American society as compared to the dominant, non-Hispanic white American group.

6. _____ refers to the number of eligible men available for women seeking marital partners.

7. In a _____ family system, the extended family and community are involved in caring for children.

8. _____ families are those in which some family members are American citizens or legal residents, while others are not legally in the United States and subject to sudden deportation.

9. Miller's typology of _____ families posited a continuum from traditional to transitional to bicultural to marginal families.

10. _____ refers to one's overall status in society.

KEY THEORETICAL PERSPECTIVES

Miller's typology of urban Native American families

INTERNET AND INFOTRAC EXERCISES

Internet Exercises

1. A great deal of controversy has been generated by President Bush's immigration plan. Go to http://www.whitehouse.gov/infocus/immigration/, where you will find Bush's Comprehensive Immigration Reform Plan. After you have read this plan, think about whether you agree or disagree with the President's stand on immigration and make a list of the major points in your personal position.

2. The *Family Research Council* is an organization devoted to preserving the "traditional" family in American society. The FRC has a decidedly conservative social agenda, and this exercise is not intended to promote support for the organization, nor to disparage it. Go to http://www.frc.org/get.cfm?c=CENTER_MARRIAGE There, you will find a variety of current concerns of this organization. Explore a few of these concerns in order to familiarize yourself with the FRC's stance on marriage and family-related concerns. Do you agree with what the FRC stands for? Do you disagree? Why?

3. As noted in this chapter, "Internet dating" is becoming more and more popular as electronic technologies proliferate in our society. *Guide to Safe Dating* is a website devoted to the discussion of issues surrounding this increasingly common practice. Go to http://www.guidetosafedating.com/ Click on several options within "Critical Information," such as "The Do's and Don'ts of Internet Dating" or "Defining the Boundaries of Internet Dating." Browse the contents of this site. If you have already experimented with Internet dating, what are your feelings about using electronic technologies in this fashion? If you haven't had any experience, would this option have any attraction for you? Why or why not?

4. Read about racially and ethnically mixed marriages in an article from the Washington Post at http://www.washingtonpost.com/wp-srv/national/daily/dec98/melt29.htm After reading the article, think about the changes in the ethnic composition of our country. What do you think will be the ethnic composition of the country in 20 years? 30 years? What changes do you think will be a part of the racial and ethnic changes?

InfoTrac Exercises

1. Use InfoTrac in order to read an article by Dana Kolesar that deals with *family surveillance*: "Intra-Family Electronic Surveillance And Access: Application Of Traditional Privacy Law And Exceptions To New Technology." The article can be easily accessed by simply typing in the author's name in the InfoTrac "Search" box.

2. Access Isabel Choat's article *Love at First Site* (type the author's name in the "Search" box), which deals with this phenomenon at eye-level. After you have read Choat's article, summarize the online dating scene.

3. The text discusses the impact of biomedical technology on the American family. Examine the issues that are discussed in this insert more closely by entering the key word "reproductive technologies" using InfoTrac. Choose two or three articles that deal with in vitro fertilization, embryo transplant, and/or surrogate parenthood. What kinds of social controversies are involved with these issues. What are your reactions to these controversies?

MULTIPLE CHOICE

1. _____   At the end of World War II in the late 1940s, which of the following changes occurred among families?
   a.   the marriage rate increased
   b.   the divorce rate increased
   c.   the baby boom ended
   d.   married couples were separated

2. _____   According to the text, the present historical moment is one of
   a.   repulsion to terrorism.
   b.   cultural revolution.
   c.   adaptation to rather profound cultural change and economic ups and downs much affected by the globalization of the economy.
   d.   turmoil.

3. _____   At the beginning of the 20th century, life expectancy was 47 years, but an American child born in 2004 is expected to live to age
   a.   67.
   b.   78.
   c.   87.
   d.   97.

4. _____   According to the text, the term *race*
   a.   does not imply a biologically distinct group.
   b.   has been documented by scientific thinking as a distinct biological marker.
   c.   is a social construction reflecting how people think about race.
   d.   is meaningless.

5. _____   *Hispanic* or *Latino* is considered a(n)
   a.   race.
   b.   racial category.
   c.   biological construction.
   d.   ethnic identity.

6. _____   *Ethnicity* refers to
   a.   culture.
   b.   biological connotations.
   c.   racial categories.
   d.   distinct genetic divisions.

7. _____   The text points out that the categories of *race, ethnicity,* and *minority group* are all
   a.   biological divisions.
   b.   genetically determined.
   c.   social constructions.
   d.   deterministic.

8. _____ Which of the following perspectives views the qualities that distinguish minority families from mainstream white families?
   a.   cultural equivalent perspective
   b.   cultural kinship perspective
   c.   cultural deviant perspective
   d.   cultural variant perspective

9. _____ _____ are now the largest minority group in the United States.
   a.   Hispanics
   b.   African Americans
   c.   Asian Americans
   d.   American Indians

10. _____ In analyzing Hispanic families, Mexican immigrants in particular have a _____ family culture.
   a.   classic
   b.   female headed
   c.   pre-nuptial
   d.   retreat from marriage

11. _____ Estimates are that there are _____ undocumented immigrants resident in the United States.
   a.   250,000
   b.   500,000
   c.   1 to 2 million
   d.   11 million

12. _____ One feature of recent immigration pointed out in the text is that immigrants may have _____ identities and families.
   a.   transnational
   b.   multicultural
   c.   undocumented
   d.   uncertain

13. _____ Families whose members have different legal statuses, with one spouse being a legal resident and the other not, are considered _____ families.
   a.   transnational
   b.   multinational
   c.   binational
   d.   multicultural

14. _____ Among the various racial/ethnic groups, the greatest diversity in terms of language, religion and customs, exists among
   a.   Hispanics
   b.   Asians
   c.   Native Americans
   d.   African Americans

15. _____ _____ are often termed a "model minority."
   a.   Mexican Americans
   b.   American Indians (Native Americans)
   c.   Asian Americans
   d.   White ethnics

16. _____ In 2006, _____ of Native Americans had incomes of more than $50,000.
   a.   one-quarter
   b.   one-third
   c.   one-half
   d.   two-thirds

17. _____ Much that is written about "the family" or "the American family" is grounded in common patterns among
   a.   middle class whites.
   b.   African Americans.
   c.   upper-class Asian Americans
   d.   Native Americans.

18. _____ According to the 2000 Census, what percent of married couple households have spouses of different racial/ethnic identities?
   a.   7%
   b.   9%
   c.   11%
   d.   15%

19. _____ Which of the following is NOT associated with religious affiliation?
   a.   married
   b.   having children
   c.   single
   d.   divorced

20. _____ Which of the following has the highest family income?
   a.   male-headed families
   b.   female-headed families
   c.   married-couple families with wives in the labor force
   d.   married-couple families in which the wife is not in the labor force

21. _____ Of all the immigrant families, the text points out that the least is known about which of the following groups?
   a.   Hispanic
   b.   Asian American
   c.   Pacific Islander
   d.   White Ethnics

22. _____ When compared to the average family in the United States, American Indians
   a.   have lower rates of fertility.
   b.   have higher numbers of single parent families.
   c.   have higher rates of religiosity.
   d.   have higher rates of cohabitation.

23. _____ In Miller's typology of urban Native American families, those who develop a blend of native beliefs and the ability to live in urban settings would be classified as
    a.   transitional families
    b.   marginal families
    c.   bicultural families
    d.   traditional families

24. _____ Which of the following groups is most likely to emphasize obedience and to use physical punishment as a part of their child rearing practices?
    a.   mainstream Protestants
    b.   Catholics
    c.   Muslims
    d.   conservative Protestants

25. _____ For Muslims, all of the following are considered religious issues EXCEPT
    a.   dating.
    b.   employment of men.
    c.   employment of women.
    d.   child rearing.

26. _____ Life chances are best defined as
    a.   chances one will live to age 75 or greater.
    b.   chances that an individual will have social security benefits.
    c.   chances that one will be able to get an education and have a good job.
    d.   chances that one will have greater than $50,000 annual income.

27. _____ Which of the following is NOT a feature of military life?
    a.   separation from family
    b.   frequent geographic relocation
    c.   suppressed individual interests
    d.   guaranteed residential stability

28. _____ In the cultural equivalent perspective, which features of families are emphasized?
    a.   those features that various racial and ethnic groups have in common
    b.   those family features distinctive of various groups
    c.   features that are related to religious values of racial and ethnic groups
    d.   features that are the least common in any group

29. _____ Which of the following is NOT a measure of social class mentioned by the text?
    a.   social status
    b.   education
    c.   occupation
    d.   income

30. _____ Families often turn to religion during times of disruption. Which of the following is not one of those events as mentioned in the text?
    a.   divorce
    b.   birth of a child
    c.   separation
    d.   remarriage

TRUE-FALSE

1. _____   According to the text, all families are alike in form.

2. _____   The income inequality gap has widened and the rich have gotten richer and the poor have gotten poorer.

3. _____   There are approximately 11 million undocumented immigrants in the United States.

4. _____   Race is a biological category rather than a social construction.

5. _____   Experts generally agree that the cause of the decline in marriage and two-parent families among African Americans is economic independence.

6. _____   Native American families have the highest rates of social problems in the United States.

7. _____   Gender roles are an area of family change that has not been shaped by immigration.

8. _____   Asian Americans have low rates of intermarriage and are more residentially segregated than other minority groups.

9. _____   Catholic fertility now parallels that of the general population.

10. _____   The 2000 median household income matches the highest ever recorded, although it declined in 2001 and 2002.

SHORT ANSWER

1.   Briefly explain what C. Wright Mills meant by the relationship between "history" and "personal biography."

2.   Briefly explain why sociologists regard *race, ethnicity,* and *minority group* as "social constructions."

3.   The text observes that African American families are *child-focused*. Briefly explain this observation.

4.   Based on the text's discussion, compare and contrast blue-collar and white-collar families.

5.   How has electronic communication technology affected American families? Give an example.

ESSAY

1. How has the age structure of American society changed over the past 100 years? Why are these changes significant for the study of marriages and families?

2. How are African American families different from white families?

3. Discuss Miller's typology of Native American families. Be sure to define each of the four categories in this continuum.

4. Discuss the unequal distribution of income in the United States. How is this significant for the study of American families?

5. Discuss the implications of reproductive and genetic technology for the members of American families. Give an example or two to support your answer.

Chapter 3

ANSWERS TO SAMPLE QUESTIONS

<u>Completion (using key terms)</u>

1.	Undocumented	6.	Sex ratio
2.	role-reversal	7.	child-focused
3.	race	8.	Binational
4.	Ethnicity	9.	Native American
5.	Minority group	10.	Social class

<u>Multiple Choice (page references in parentheses)</u>

1.	b (48)	16.	b (66)
2.	c (48)	17.	a (37)
3.	b (49)	18.	c (38)
4.	c (54)	19.	d (38)
5.	d (55)	20.	c (45)
6.	a (55)	21.	c (65)
7.	c (55)	22.	d (66)
8.	c (57)	23.	c (67)
9.	a (58)	24.	d (71)
10.	c (61)	25	b (71)
11.	d (62)	26.	c (49)
12.	a (62)	27.	d (50)
13.	c (62)	28.	a (52)
14.	b (64)	29.	a (53)
15.	c (64)	30.	c (70)

<u>True-False (page references in parentheses)</u>

1.	F (48)	6.	T (65)
2.	T (52)	7.	F (64)
3.	T (62)	8.	F (64)
4.	F (54)	9.	T (70)
5.	F (59)	10.	T (67)

CHAPTER 4

OUR GENDERED IDENTITIES

CHAPTER SUMMARY

Gender influences people's behavior, attitudes, and options. **Gender identity** refers to the degree to which an individual sees herself or himself as feminine or masculine, based on society's definitions of appropriate gender roles. In the dominant culture of the United States, women tend to be seen as more expressive, relationship-oriented, "communal", and as having more **communal** or **expressive character traits**; men tend to be considered more **agentic** and as having more **instrumental character traits**.

There are racial/ethnic variations in gender expectations. **"Traditional sexism"** has declined since the 1970s, but now a more subtle **"modern sexism"** is often evident. Generally, traditional masculine expectations require that men be confident, self-reliant, and occupationally successful and engage in "no sissy stuff." During the 1980s, the "new male" (or "liberated male") cultural message emerged, where men are expected to value tenderness and equal relationships with women. Traditional feminine expectations involve a woman being a man's help-mate and a "good mother." An emergent feminine role is the successful "professional woman;" when coupled with the more traditional ones, this results in the "superwoman." The extent to which men and women differ from one another and follow these cultural messages can be visualized as two overlapping normal distribution curves. The statistical "means" differ according to cultural expectations, but within-group variation is usually greater than between-group variation. Put in non-statistical terms, this simply means that there is more variation among males as a group and among women as a group than there is when males as a group are compared with females as a group. On an interpersonal level, **male dominance** describes a situation in which the male(s) in a dyad or group assume authority over the female(s). Male dominance may be seen in the realms of politics, religion, and the economy.

Biology interacts with culture to produce human behavior, and the two influences are difficult to separate. Sociologists give greater attention to the socialization process, for which there are several theoretical explanations. The most developed biosocial gender theory is that of demographer J. Richard Udry. In arguing against a biological determinism of whatever sort, sociologists point to instances in which gender-expected behaviors have followed no logical pattern based on biological differences. Very probably, biology and society interact to create **gender-linked characteristics and roles**.

Social structure and societal values influence how we behave. The process by which society influences members to internalize attitudes and expectations is **socialization**. Our cultural images in language and in the media convey gendered expectations. There are a number of competing theories of gendered socialization: *social learning, self-identification, gender schema,* and *Chodorow's theory of gender.* Parents rear girls and boys differently. Boys and girls tend to play separately and differently. Schools socialize males and females differently, to include differences in social organization, teachers' practices, and programs. College environments tend to be more liberating, but there are still some instances of inequality. In the last several years, attention has been turned to boys and some attack the "myth of girls in crisis."

One of the most dramatic changes of the last thirty years has been the rapid shift in what the culture expects of men and women. Traditional gender roles result in some characteristic stresses. Sometimes, in response to these stresses, adults reconsider earlier choices regarding gender roles. These choices are illustrated by Kathleen Gerson's research on women's and men's roles choices. New options have been presented to women through the women's movement. As the women's movement encouraged changes in gendered cultural expectations and social organization, some men responded by initiating a men's movement. Kimmel has divided today's men's movement into three fairly distinct camps: *antifeminists, profeminists,* and *masculinists.* **Androgyny** is the social and psychological condition by which individuals think, feel, and behave both instrumentally and expressively. Feminists have disagreed about androgyny as a model for women.

LEARNING OBJECTIVES

Based on your careful and thorough reading of Chapter 4, you should:

1. be familiar with the gender expectations in our society and the cultural expectations that men and women confront.

2. understand the distinction between traditional and modern sexism.

3. be familiar with the history of male dominance and patriarchy.

4. be able to distinguish between biologically based and society-based arguments regarding sex and gender, and understand the interaction of culture and biology.

5. be familiar with the different theories of gender socialization.

6. understand the significance of gender in men's and women's adult lives, including the relationships between gender and stress and between gender and personal change.

7. be familiar with the impact of the women's movement and the men's movement.

8. understand the significance of androgyny in terms of women's and men's roles in society.

KEY TERMS (page references in parentheses)

agentic (instrumental) character traits (78)
borderwork (89)
Chodorow's theory of gender (88)
communal (expressive) character traits (78)
femininities (79)
gender (76)
gender identity (76)
gender role (76)
gender schema theory of gender socialization (87)
gender similarities hypothesis (81)
hormonal processes (86)
hormones (86)
intersexual (78)
male dominance (81)

masculinities (78)
modern sexism (77)
play (89)
self-identification theory of gender socialization (93)
sex (76)
social learning theory of gender socialization (87)
socialization (87)
symbolic interaction theory of gender socialization (88)
traditional sexism (77)
transgendered (78)
transsexual (78)

COMPLETION (using key terms)

1. _____ refers to male or female anatomy or physiology.

2. _____ refers to the degree to which an individual sees herself or himself as feminine or masculine based on society's definitions of appropriate gender roles.

3. Competitiveness, self-confidence, logic, and nonemotionality as allegedly "natural" for men are examples of _____ character traits.

4. _____ character traits are perceived to be more "feminine," and include sensitivity to the needs of others and the ability to express tender feelings.

5. All men are not alike. That is why it makes sense to speak of _____.

6. The concepts of "good mother," "professional woman," and "superwoman" are examples of _____.

7. In politics, religion, and in the economy, there is evidence of _____ – a situation in which the male(s) in a dyad or group assume authority over the female(s).

8. _____ sexism refers to believing that women's roles should be confined to family roles (wife, mother) and that women are not as fit as men for certain tasks or for leadership positions at home or in the world.

9. _____ sexism denies that gender discrimination persists and believes that women are probably asking too much now.

10. The term _____ describes an identity adopted by those who are uncomfortable in the gender of their birth.

11. An individual who wants to have surgery to have their body conform to their gender identity is a _____.

12. Approximately one to four percent of individuals who have anatomical, chromosomal, or hormonal variations are referred to as being _____.

13. Some psychologists think that what comes first is not rules about what boys and girls should do, but rather the child's awareness of being a boy or a girl. This statement is consistent with _____ theory.

14. _____ theory posits that children develop a framework of knowledge about what girls and boys typically do.

15. The role of _____ is a vehicle through which children develop appropriate concepts of adult roles.

KEY THEORETICAL PERSPECTIVES

biological theories of gender differences
Udry's biosocial gender theory
Huber's theory of gender stratification
social learning theory
self-identification theory
gender schema theory
Chodorow's theory of gender

INTERNET AND INFOTRAC EXERCISES

Internet Exercises

1.   You are probably aware of the women's suffrage movement, but did you know that women did not gain the right to vote until 1920? The chances are good that you have a relatively hazy picture of the history of this movement and its significance for women's rights in contemporary American society. The following address will provide you with a brief history of women's suffrage and bring the issues into perspective: http://www.rochester.edu/SBA/suffragehistory.html. After you have familiarized yourself with the contents of this site, respond to the following questions:

   •   Given that it has been less than 100 years since women gained the right to vote, are you surprised by the progress that has been made toward gender equality? If you are female, consider what it would be like to "think about what you want to be when you grow up" and confront one obstacle after another. For example, suppose you would like to be a physician: Society responds, "That door is not open...consider being a nurse." Or, you are thinking about being a lawyer: Society responds, "Sorry…even if you manage to earn a law degree and pass the Bar, there isn't a law firm in existence that will hire you." Of course, these conditions were present in our society long after 1920. But, women's suffrage was the beginning. If you are male, do you feel intimidated in any way by the women's rights movement? Why or why not?

   •   Do you think a woman will be President of the United States? When do you think this will happen?

2.   The National Organization for Women (NOW) is the largest organization of feminist activists in the United States. Go to the following website in order to obtain a detailed history of this organization: http://www.now.org/history/history.html There, you will find discussions of the organization's views on sexual harassment and violence, abortion rights and reproductive freedom, lesbian rights, women's work, and how NOW functions as an organization representing the rights of women. After you have perused the materials within this website, respond to the following questions:

   •   If it were not for the activities of NOW during the last three decades of the twentieth century, how do you think women's rights would be viewed in the early twenty-first century?

   •   Compare the activities of NOW with similar organizations that have represented minority racial groups, such as the NAACP. In this regard, you may wish to visit their official website: http://www.naacp.org/

3.   In most divorce situations, mothers are granted primary custody of dependent children. Men are most likely to become "non-custodial" parents and to be granted "visitation" with their children. Within the men's movement, a number of outspoken critics have argued that it is insulting for a parent to be referred to as a "visitor" with respect to his/her children. The Alliance for Non-Custodial Parents' Rights http://www.ancpr.org/ is an organization devoted to helping fathers to gain equal rights when it comes to their position as a parent in divorce situations. Go to this website and take a look at some of the "current contents." You will find a number of "headline issues" highlighted, which will help you to gain a better understanding of one of the key components of the men's movement today. After you have explored this site, respond to the following questions:

- Do you think that men are discriminated against in divorce situations as far as the child custody issue is concerned? Why or why not?
- Stories about "Deadbeat Dads" (fathers who fail to pay their court-ordered child support) are legion. But what about mothers who deny or otherwise complicate the process involving their ex-husbands' "visitation" with their dependent children? Should mothers be disciplined by the court for this kind of behavior? Why or why not?
- Do you think that we continue to view mothers as the "main character" in terms of parenting? Is this a form of discrimination against men in their role as fathers? Why or why not?

4.   Go to the National Women's Law Center at http://www.nwlc.org/display.cfm?section=employment and click on issues. Read about issues affecting gender roles and women such as Gender Equity, Child Care and Early Education and Workplace Fairness and Flexibility.

After reading about several of these issues, do you feel that the old saying "we've come a long way, baby" applies to women?

Have the benefits for women in the workforce benefited men as well?

InfoTrac Exercises

1.   Use the key phrase *patriarchy and gender*. You will find numerous articles dealing with this subject. Select two or three that deal directly with the relationship between patriarchy and gender. Read the articles and respond to these questions:

- How do you think the tradition of patriarchy has affected gender roles and relationships between men and women in American society?
- No doubt, the women's movement has had a measurable impact on patriarchy over the past three decades, but there is also no denying that the tradition is still operating today. Make a list of the ways in which patriarchy is still "alive and well."
- Do you think the patriarchal tradition will ever disappear? Why or why not?

2.   Use the key phrase, *gender and language*, which will generate a large number of citations. There are a number of interesting articles concerning the relationship between language and gender. Pick two or three and read them for content. Then, respond to the following questions:

- The textbook provides a number of examples of how language is related to gender roles and our perceptions of males and females in society. Write a short essay recording what else you learned about language and gender from reading these articles.

- The text points to a recent edition of Webster's College Dictionary that provides definitions for new words, such as *waitron* (gender-neutral for "waiter") and *womyn* (intended to avoid the perception of sexism in the word "men"). Do you think that this is an effective technique to encourage gender equality in terms of language? Why or why not?
- The text points out that a new mother may be told that she has either a *"lovely girl"* or a *"strong boy."* These language-based gender stereotypes are common in American society. Make a list of similar linguistic expressions that perpetuate such stereotypes. Did the InfoTrac articles you selected discuss gender stereotypes in the language? If so, what did you learn?

3. Use the key phrase, *the men's movement*. This will produce a large number of citations. Browse through the articles that are available. Choose two or three of these articles and peruse them. Then, respond to the following questions:
   - What are the similarities and differences between the men's movement and the women's movement in American society?
   - Do you think that men need to be represented by an organization like the National Organization for Women (NOW)? Why or why not?
   - Do you think that the men's movement will continue to flourish or eventually fade from view? What is the basis for your judgment in this regard?

MULTIPLE CHOICE

1. _____ Jack believes that a woman's "place" is in the home. Jack's point of view is an illustration of _____ sexism.
   a. modern
   b. neo
   c. traditional
   d. post-modern

2. _____ Consider the statement "Discrimination against women in the labor force is no longer a problem." This reflects _____ sexism.
   a. neo
   b. modern
   c. traditional
   d. post-modern

3. _____ Which term is used to describe societal attitudes and behaviors expected of and associated with the two sexes?
   a. sex
   b. gender
   c. intersexuality
   d. transsexualities

4. _____ Stereotypically masculine people are often thought to have _____ character traits.
   a. communal or expressive
   b. machismo
   c. agentic or instrumental
   d. diverse

5. _____   _____ persons have some anatomical, chromosomal, or hormonal variation from the male or female biology that is considered "normal."
   a.   Intersexual
   b.   Transgendered
   c.   Transsexual
   d.   Homosexual

6. _____   Which of the following is NOT one of the cultural messages for men?
   a.   defend his pride
   b.   support his family
   c.   stand up for his family
   d.   express emotional feelings

7. _____   Suppose we are comparing height differences among men. This reflects which category of variation?
   a.   within-group
   b.   between-group
   c.   outside-group
   d.   external-group

8. _____   In which of the following religious categories are women prohibited from holding positions?
   a.   the pastorate within Protestant Christian churches
   b.   rabbis in Reform Jewish congregations
   c.   feminist evangelicals
   d.   Catholic clerical or lay deacon

9. _____   Biological theories of gender difference were initially offered by
   a.   biologists.
   b.   primatologists.
   c.   zoologists.
   d.   geneticists.

10. _____   Most contemporary biologists are focusing on _____ to explain gender differences.
   a.   hormones
   b.   brain lateralization
   c.   evolution
   d.   psychology

11. _____   Women tend to choose jobs that are lower paying for all of the following reasons EXCEPT
   a.   emotionally satisfying
   b.   flexible scheduling
   c.   offers opportunities for upward mobility
   d.   compatible with childbearing

12. _____   _____ is a form of social organization based on the supremacy of fathers and inheritance through the male line.
   a.   Sexism
   b.   Gender hierarchy
   c.   Gender stratification
   d.   Patriarchy

13. _____   The socialization process is an important concept in which of the following perspectives?
- a. interactional
- b. structural functional
- c. conflict
- d. exchange

14. _____   _____ theory posits that children develop a framework of knowledge about what girls and boys typically do.
- a. Functional
- b. Conflict
- c. Gender schema
- d. Exchange

15. _____   According to the text, girls' toys
- a. develop spatial ability and creative construction.
- b. elicit closer physical proximity and more talk between child and caregiver.
- c. encourage physical activity.
- d. encourage independent play.

16. _____   Researchers who observed more than 100 fourth-, sixth-, and eighth-grade classes over a three-year period found that
- a. teachers called on girls more often than boys.
- b. teachers encouraged girls more than boys.
- c. boys consistently and clearly dominated classrooms.
- d. none of the above

17. _____   Chicano/Chicana (Mexican American) activism gave _____ a central place as a distinctive cultural value.
- a. machismo
- b. la familia
- c. children
- d. parents

18. _____   Which of the following is NOT one of Kimmel's fairly distinct camps of today's men's movement?
- a. antifeminists
- b. profeminists
- c. equal rights enthusiasts
- d. masculinists

19. _____   Robert Bly's *Iron John* is a prominent example of which camp?
- a. "masculinist"
- b. "antifeminist"
- c. "profeminist"
- d. "androgynist"

20. _____   Sociologist Stephen Nock expects marriages of the future to be
- a. male dominated
- b. codependent
- c. female dominated
- d. equally dependent

21. _____ Modern sexism is characterized by all of the following statements EXCEPT
    a.   discrimination in the labor force is non-existent
    b.   men and women are different in personality and opportunity
    c.   gender discrimination persists
    d.   men are inclined to overcompensate women to appear nonsexist

22. _____ The gender similarities hypothesis focuses on
    a.   assumptions about gender difference from the 1970s research.
    b.   the fact that men and women are more alike than they are different.
    c.   the tendencies of males toward aggressive behavior.
    d.   socialization that is based on inequalities.

23. _____ The number of women in college is
    a.   greater than the number of men.
    b.   less than the number of men.
    c.   is equal to the number of men.
    d.   had not changed significantly since 1979.

24. _____ Genetic heritage is expressed through
    a.   psychological forces.
    b.   hormonal processes.
    c.   socialization.
    d.   cultural transmission.

25. _____ Gender schema theory is most similar to which of the following theories?
    a.   symbolic interactionism
    b.   social learning
    c.   self identification
    d.   Chodorow's theory

26. _____ Which of the following theorists is associated with the development of children's self-concept through role-taking?
    a.   Eleanor Macoby
    b.   Nancy Chodorow
    c.   Robert Merton
    d.   George Herbert Mead

27. _____ Parents differentiate between girls and boys through
    a.   types of discipline.
    b.   allocation of household chores.
    c.   providing identical play groups.
    d.   privileges.

28. _____ In schools where there are sexual interaction rituals, these are referred to as
    a.   gender socialization.
    b.   agentic socialization.
    c.   borderwork.
    d.   care work.

29. _____ Research to determine if girls are channeled into or avoid traditionally masculine courses in high school found all of the following EXCEPT
   a. boys and girls take similar numbers of science courses.
   b. girls enroll in more AP courses.
   c. girls take more computer courses.
   d. girls cluster in traditional female occupations.

30. _____ The Women's Movement of the 1920s is noted because it resulted in
   a. equal pay for equal work.
   b. 40 hour work week for women in factories.
   c. women's right to vote.
   d. guaranteed health benefits.

TRUE-FALSE

1. _____ Although gender expectations have changed and continue to change, they have obviously not done so completely.

2. _____ The text points out that men are not all alike.

3. _____ The preeminence of the male provider role is a powerful theme in all racial/ethnic groups.

4. _____ Unlike the family, religion does not display male dominance.

5. _____ All male primates are dominant and aggressive.

6. _____ Macoby sees boy's rough play, earlier separation from adults and poor impulse control as being biologically based.

7. _____ Children's television programming more often depicts boys than girls in dominant, agentic roles.

8. _____ Research shows that teachers pay more attention to males than females.

9. _____ African American women and men are more likely than whites to endorse political organizing for women's issues.

10. _____ Women are very consistent in their attitudes toward the women's movement.

11. _____ Research suggests that "post-feminism" is a myth.

12. _____ The newer masculinists tend not to focus on patriarchy as problematic.

13. _____ The "new man" is expected to succeed economically and to value relationships and emotional openness.

14. _____ Profeminists support feminism and patriarchy.

15. _____ Marriages of equally dependent spouses represent the future of American marriages.

SHORT ANSWER

1.   To what extent do individual men and women fit gender stereotypes and expectations?

2.   If males dominate in the political sphere – and they do – what ways and by what mechanisms do they dominate?

3.   Summarize the ways in which play and games are related to socialization to gender expectations, identifies, and roles.

4.   According to the text, what has been the response of black women about committing themselves to feminist goals?

5.   Distinguish between "masculinists" and "anti-feminists."

ESSAY QUESTIONS

1.   What are the origins of gender differences and inequalities according to society-based explanations? Be specific and support your answer with such facts as help to enhance the persuasiveness of your essay.

2.   In an organized, well-written essay, explore how culture and biology interact to produce, intensify, and perpetuate gender differences. Support your essay with specific terms, theories, and research results wherever possible and appropriate.

3.   Distinguish between social learning theory and self-identification theory of acquiring gender attitudes, expectations, and behaviors. In your essay, be sure to point out the similarities and differences of these two explanations.

4.   According to the text, schools help perpetuate and intensify gender attitudes and expectations. Write an essay in which you explore how the factors mentioned in textbook seem evident at the college or university in which you are enrolled. Be specific, using terms appropriately and citing research results where appropriate to support the ideas in your essay.

5.   Select one of the following minority groups and write an essay in which you summarize the chapter's information about that minority group and gender realities: African American women, or Hispanic women (Latinas, Chicanas).

ANSWERS TO SAMPLE QUESTIONS

Completion (using key terms)

1.	Sex	9.	Modern
2.	Gender identity	10.	transgendered
3.	agentic or instrumental	11.	transsexual
4.	communal or expressive	12.	Social learning
5.	masculinities	13.	intersexual
6.	femininities	14.	Gender schema
7.	male dominance	15.	play
8.	Traditional		

Multiple Choice (page references in parentheses)

1.	c (77)	16.	c (90)
2.	b (78)	17.	b (93)
3.	b (76)	18.	c (95)
4.	c (78)	19.	a (96)
5.	a (78)	20.	d (97)
6.	d (79)	21.	c (78)
7.	a (78)	22.	b (81)
8.	d (82)	23.	a (83)
9.	b (85)	24.	b (86)
10.	a (86)	25.	b (87-88)
11.	c (85)	26.	d (88)
12.	d (81)	27.	b (89)
13.	a (88)	28.	c (89)
14.	c (87)	29.	c (91)
15.	b (89)	30.	c (93}

True-False (page references in parentheses)

1.	T (78)	9.	T (92)
2.	T (78-79)	10.	F (93)
3.	T (80)	11.	T (94)
4.	F (82)	12.	F (95)
5.	F (87)	13.	T (96)
6.	T (89)	14.	F (95)
7.	T (89)	15.	T (97)
8.	T (90)		

CHAPTER 5

LOVING OURSELVES AND OTHERS

CHAPTER SUMMARY

In an impersonal society, **love** provides an important source of fulfillment and intimacy. Genuine loving in our society is rare and difficult to learn. Most people search for at least one caring person with whom to share their private time. Love is a deep and vital **emotion**. Love satisfies legitimate personal needs. Love involves caring and acceptance. Love involves **intimacy** and a **commitment** to sharing. Both **psychic** and **sexual intimacy** are involved here. Loving and being loved have important consequences for emotional and physical well-being.

In the **triangular theory of love**, Sternberg uses the three dimensions of **intimacy**, **passion** and **commitment** to generate a typology of love, one of which types, called **consummate love**, involves all three compone nts. John Lee lists six love styles: **eros**, or passionate love; **storge**, or companionate, familiar love; **pragma**, or pragmatic love; **agape** or altruistic love; **ludus** or love play; and **mania** or possessive love.

Despite its importance, however, love is often misunderstood. It should not be confused with **martyring** or **manipulating**. There are many contemporary love styles that indicate the range of dimensions love-like relationships – not necessarily love – can take. **Self-esteem** seems to be a prerequisite for loving. In relationships where there is emotional **interdependence**, love probably involves acceptance of oneself and others, a sense of empathy, and a willingness to let down barriers set up for self-preservation. **A-frame**, **H-frame**, and **M-frame** relationships are some of the forms love can take. Attachment theory holds that during infancy and childhood a young person develops a general style of attaching to others. There are three basic styles of attachment: **secure, insecure/anxious,** and **avoidant**. People discover love; they don't simply find it or have it strike like a thunderbolt. Put differently, love is not an event; love is an unfolding process. Reiss's **wheel theory of love** sets forth four basic stages of the love process: **rapport**, **self-disclosure, mutual dependency**, and personal need **fulfillment.**

Since partners need to keep on sharing their thoughts, feelings, troubles, and joys with each other, love is a continual process. Discovering love implies a process, and to develop and maintain a loving relationship requires mutual **self-disclosure**, requiring time and trust. Mutual dependency and personality need fulfillment are also part of the "wheel of love." Various misconceptions may limit our ability to maintain love. Infatuation is but a beginning. Love is not perfect; it does not conquer all; and **being realistic** is important. **Mutuality** refers to both partners meeting one another's needs. Love involves much more than a feeling.

LEARNING OBJECTIVES

Based on your careful and thorough reading of Chapter 5, you should:

1.   be familiar with the characteristics of love.

2.   understand the distinction between legitimate and illegitimate needs, and between psychic and sexual intimacy.

3.   be familiar with Sternberg's triangular theory of love.

4.   be familiar with Lee's six love styles: *eros, storge, pragma, agape, ludus,* and *mania.*

5.   understand the two things love *isn't.*

6.   understand self-worth (self-esteem) as a prerequisite to loving and the distinction between self-love and narcissism.

7.   understand emotional interdependence, dependence, and independence.

8.   be familiar with the different attachment styles.

9.   understand love as a discovery.

10.   be familiar with Reiss's wheel theory of love.

11.   understand the dynamics involved with keeping love.

KEY TERMS (page references in parentheses)

A-frame relationships (112)
agape (108)
attachment theory (113)
avoidant attachment style (113)
co-dependent (110)
commitment (104)
commitment [Sternberg's theory] (105)
consummate love (105)
dependence (111)
emotion (103)
eros (107)
H-frame relationships (113)
illegitimate needs (103)
independence (112)
insecure/anxious attachment style (113)
interdependence (112)
intimacy (104)
intimacy [Sternberg's theory] (105)
legitimate needs (103)
love (102)
love styles (107)

ludus (108)
mania (108)
manipulating (109)
martyring (109)
mutuality (116)
M-frame relationships (113)
Mutuality (116)
narcissism (116)
passion [Sternberg's theory] (105)
pragma (108)
psychic intimacy (104)
secure attachment style (113)
self-disclosure (114)
self revelation (114)
self-worth (self-esteem) (110)
sexual intimacy (104)
Sternberg's triangular theory of love (105)
storge (107)
symbiotic relationships (110)
wheel of love (114)

COMPLETION (using key terms)

1. A(n) _____ is a strong feeling, arising without conscious mental or rational effort, that motivates an individual to behave in a certain way.

2. _____ are those arising in the present rather than out of deficits or failures accumulated in the past.

3. _____ spring from feelings of self-doubt, unworthiness, and inadequacy.

4. According to Sternberg's triangular theory of love, when intimacy, passion, and commitment are all involved, the result is the type of love called _____.

5. _____ refer to the various distinctive "personalities" that love-like relationships can take.

6. The type of love that is characterized by intense emotional attachment and powerful sexual feelings or desires is termed _____.

7. The term _____ refers to an affectionate, companionate style of loving.

8. _____ is the kind of love involving an emphasis on the practical side of human relationships, emphasizing economic and emotional security.

9. Often called altruistic love, _____ emphasizes unselfish concern for the beloved.

10. The type of love that emphasizes playfulness and the humorous or amusing aspects of the love relationship is what is meant by _____.

11. An insatiable need for attention and affection alternating between euphoria and depression is characteristic of a _____ love style.

12. _____ involves maintaining relationships by giving others more than one receives in return, usually with good intentions, but seldom with the feeling that genuine affection is being received.

13. _____ means seeking to control the feelings, attitudes, and behavior of the partner by subtle, indirect ways rather than by straightforwardly stating one's case or position about the matter at hand.

14. Martyrs and manipulators are often attracted to each other, forming what counselor John Crosby calls a(n) _____.

15. _____ refers to an evaluation a person makes and maintains of herself or himself that expresses attitudes of approval or disapproval, success or failure, worth or unworthiness, and similar ideas.

16. _____ is essentially another word for selfishness.

17. The concept of _____ refers to a general reliance on another person or on other people for continual support or assurance, along with subordination.

18. The first stage in the wheel theory of the development of love is _____.

19. _____ refers to self-reliance, self-sufficiency, sometimes including separation or isolation from others.

20. When we label a relationship _____, we imply that the people involved have high self-esteem and make strong commitments to each other.

21. In _____ relationships, the partners stand self-sufficient and virtually alone, with neither influenced much by the other.

22. In _____, each partner has high self-esteem, experiences loving as deep emotion, and is involved in mutual influence and emotional support.

23. The stages of rapport, self-disclosure, mutual dependence, and personality need fulfillment and characterize the _____.

24. _____ refers to both partners meeting one another's needs.

25. _____ means that you don't expect your partner to meet *all* of your needs *all of the time*.

26. _____ are persons who gravitate toward relationships with exploitative or abusive partners around whom they organize their lives and to whom they remain strongly committed despite the absence of any identifiable rewards or personal fulfillment for themselves.

KEY THEORETICAL PERSPECTIVES

Sternberg's triangular theory of love
Lee's six love styles
Crosby's three types of interdependence relationships
attachment theory
Reiss' wheel theory of love

INTERNET AND INFOTRAC EXERCISES

Internet Exercises

1. There are countless numbers of "personal compatibility quizzes" that are accessible through various websites on the Internet. Of course, many of these are highly commercialized and of questionable value. At the same time, there is something to be learned about the components of intimate relationships from examining such inventories more closely. Using an Internet search engine (Yahoo, Google, Alta Vista, Ask, Excite, etc.), enter the key words, "personal compatibility quizzes." Take a look at two or three of these inventories. After you have done this, respond to the following questions:
   - What are the central features of "love" and/or "personal compatibility" quizzes/inventories?
   - Do you think that such inventories are of any practical value? Why or why not?

2.   Electronic communication and the Internet have taken "matchmaking" and "dating services" to an entirely different level. In order to capture a glimpse of this electronic "matchmaking" environment, utilize a search engine (Ask, Google, Yahoo, etc.) to locate websites that offer these services. All you have to do is plug in the keyword "matchmaking." After you have explored a few of these sites, answer these questions:

- What do you think are the pros and cons of "matchmaking services?" Would you participate in a program of this type? Why or why not?
- Why do you think that some American men are interested in forming a relationship with women from other countries (Russia, the Ukraine, etc.)? Do European women look at love differently than American women?

3.   After having visited several of the dating or matchmaking sites, go to www.eharmony.com and to www.chemistry.com. Read about the services that each offers.

How do their services differ? How do they compare in terms of costs? If you were going to use a matchmaking service, which one would you prefer and why?

Finally, go to www.datingwebsitecomparisons.com and see how different sites are ranked.

4.   This is far from scientific, and it's just for fun, but will serve as a partial illustration of John Lee's six Styles of Love: *eros, storge, pragma, agape, ludus,* and *mania.* Go to: http://www.vietfun.com/love/. Take the "Love Psychic" quiz and submit your answers. See how you "rank" with respect to the six love styles. Then, respond to these questions:

- Do you think your profile is "accurate," given what you know about yourself?
- Do "quizzes" of this kind have any utility, or are they pure "fantasy?"

InfoTrac Exercises

1.   Try entering the keywords *love, analysis.* A variety of articles will appear. Examine as many of the sources as you feel you have time for. Respond to the following questions:

- What are the major questions that have been posed about human beings' experiences with love?
- If you were a researcher, what question would you want to analyze in reference to the phenomenon of love?

2.   Enter the keyword *intimacy.* Take a look at a few of these articles. Summarize what you have learned and respond to these questions:

- The text distinguishes between *psychic* and *sexual intimacy.* Did you learn anything further about this distinction by reading these articles? What?
- What is the relationship between *intimacy* and *alienation*?

3.   The text points out that self-worth (self-esteem) is a prerequisite to loving. Plug in the keyword *self-worth* or *self-esteem.* Select and review a few articles that deal with core demographic issues, such as *gender.* Respond to these questions:

- What are some of the self-worth/self-esteem differences between men and women?
- Do you think these differences help to explain the variations in how men and women respond to love? If so, how?

MULTIPLE CHOICE

1. _____ The text defines love as a
    a. primarily sexual phenomenon.
    b. deep and vital emotion that satisfies certain needs.
    c. relationship that may or may not be intimate.
    d. all of the above

2. _____ According to the text, achieving a sense of individuality and personal identity is a step that
    a. best precedes relationship formation.
    b. usually follows relationship formation.
    c. necessarily precedes adulthood.
    d. should take place in early childhood.

3. _____ Research indicates that
    a. women verbally express feelings of love less than men do.
    b. women's socialization has been directed more strongly to autonomy than attachment.
    c. women today do not believe that they should be more self-sacrificing in relationships.
    d. in comparison with men, women tend to be more often baffled by questions about inner feelings.

4. _____ Research on married couples indicates that partners who are self-disclosing and openly express feelings of love to each other
    a. are more likely to divorce in comparison with those who are less willing to engage in these behaviors.
    b. perceive their marriages to be more intimate and score high on measures of marital adjustment.
    c. usually lose trust in each other in the later years of their marriages.
    d. none of the above

5. _____ At the level of _____ intimacy, people engage in self-disclosure; they share their thoughts, feelings, and goals.
    a. sexual
    b. emotional
    c. marital
    d. psychic

6. _____ The drives that lead to romance, physical attraction, sexual consummation, and the like in a loving relationship are referred to in the text as
    a. passion.
    b. commitment.
    c. intimacy.
    d. consummate love.

7. _____ Which of the following consists of two aspects—one short-term and one long-term?
    a. consummate love
    b. commitment
    c. intimacy
    d. passion

8. _____ Psychologist and marriage counselor Gary Smalley argues that a couple is typically together for about _____ year(s) before they feel safe enough to share their deepest relational needs with one another.
   a. one
   b. two
   c. four
   d. six

9. _____ One of John Lee's "love styles" is _____, which is a Greek word meaning "love."
   a. pragma
   b. agape
   c. storge
   d. eros

10. _____ Which of John Lee's "love styles" focuses on deepening mutual commitment, respect, friendship over time, and common goals?
    a. storge
    b. ludus
    c. eros
    d. pragma

11. _____ Which of John Lee's "love styles" involves rational assessment of a potential partner's assets and liabilities?
    a. agape
    b. ludus
    c. pragma
    d. storge

12. _____ Which of John Lee's "love styles" emphasizes unselfish concern for the beloved's needs even when that means some personal sacrifice?
    a. pragma
    b. agape
    c. ludus
    d. mania

13. _____ "I enjoy playing the game of love with a number of different partners." This is a question designed to measure which of John Lee's "styles of love?"
    a. ludus
    b. agape
    c. mania
    d. storge

14. _____ According to John Lee's typology of "love styles," _____ lovers alternate between euphoria and depression.
    a. ludus
    b. agape
    c. storge
    d. mania

15. _____ _____ may ask others to do things for them that they could do for themselves, and generally expect to be waited on.
    a. Martyrs
    b. Narcissists
    c. Manipulators
    d. Ludic lovers

16. _____ The text points out that (a) healthy _____ results from actual, real accomplishments, not simply from hearing or telling oneself that one is, for example, "special."
    a. self-worth (self-esteem)
    b. psyche
    c. personality
    d. socialization

17. _____ The text points out that _____ are concerned chiefly with themselves, without regard for the well-being of others.
    a. ludic lovers
    b. agapic lovers
    c. narcissists
    d. dependent individuals

18. _____ John is self-reliant, self-sufficient, and functions in relative isolation from others. Based on the text's discussion, we can reasonably conclude that John is
    a. a martyr.
    b. a manipulator.
    c. dependent.
    d. independent.

19. _____ According to John Crosby's typology, _____ relationships are structured so that "if one lets go, the other falls."
    a. A-frame
    b. H-frame
    c. M-frame
    d. Agapic

20. _____ A(n) _____ attachment style would likely be evidenced in partners engaged in an A-frame or dependent relationship.
    a. secure
    b. insecure/anxious
    c. avoidant
    d. intimate

21. _____ A(n) _____ attachment style would characterize partners in an independent, or H-frame relationship.
    a. avoidant
    b. intimate
    c. secure
    d. insecure/anxious

22. _____ "Rapport," "self-revelation," "mutual dependency," and "personality need fulfillment" are the four stages in Ira Reiss's _____ theory of love.
   a. triangular
   b. love-style
   c. framework
   d. wheel

23. _____ The text points out that even for people with adequate self-esteem, loving produces
   a. anxiety.
   b. tremendous pain.
   c. enormous depression.
   d. insurmountable anger.

24. _____ The wheel theory of love suggests that once people fall in love, they
   a. will stay in love.
   b. may not necessarily stay in love.
   c. will inevitably "fall out of love."
   d. will eventually experience a reduction in love.

25. _____ Psychologist Gary Smalley alludes to "constantly recharging your mate's 'needs battery.'" In this analogy, Smalley is referring to
   a. self-disclosure.
   b. realism.
   c. mutuality.
   d. intimacy.

26. _____ The Triangular Theory of Love is based on the research of
   a. Erich Fromm.
   b. Rollo May.
   c. Robert Sternberg.
   d. Gary Smalley.

27. _____ Which of the following best describes manipulating in a relationship?
   a. one partner has a strong sexual attraction to the other
   b. one where one partner seeks to control the feelings, attitudes and behavior of the other
   c. one partner ignores their own legitimate needs
   d. one partner is totally devoted to a recreational sexual relationship

28. _____ Which of the following is found in loving relationships?
   a. martyring
   b. manipulating
   c. controlling
   d. compromising

29. _____ When someone fantasizes about another person in all kinds of romantic situations, this is called
   a. lust.
   b. limerance.
   c. puppy love.
   d. fascination.

30. _____   A relationship that is characterized by the expectation that the partner provide a sense of meaning is best described as
                 a.   dependent.
                 b.   symbiotic.
                 c.   interdependent.
                 d.   nurturing.

31. _____   Which of the following is NOT a style of attachment identified in attachment theory?
                 a.   secure
                 b.   insecure/anxious
                 c.   confident
                 d.   avoidant

32. _____   In Reiss's theory, which stage is the first in the development of a loving relationship?
                 a.   self-revelation
                 b.   mutual dependency
                 c.   rapport
                 d.   personality need fulfillment

33. _____   Which of the following hormones has been nicknamed the "love" or "cuddle" hormone?
                 a.   dopamine
                 b.   testosterone
                 c.   oxytocin
                 d.   estrogen

34. _____   The willingness to work through problems and conflicts rather than calling it quits is the definition of
                 a.   consummate love.
                 b.   psychic intimacy.
                 c.   commitment.
                 d.   passionate love.

35. _____   Consummate love, according to Sternberg, is a combination of all of the following EXCEPT
                 a.   intimacy.
                 b.   commitment.
                 c.   passion.
                 d.   limerance.

TRUE-FALSE

1. _____   Many psychologists insist that loving is essential for emotional survival.

2. _____   The text points out that if loving is sufficient, a person can be convinced that he or she is worthwhile and lovable, even if that person does not believe it.

3. _____   Psychologist Erich Fromm chastises Americans for their emphasis on wanting to *be loved* rather than on learning to *love*.

4. _____ It is possible that as gender roles change generally, men and women will develop more balanced capacities for autonomy and intimacy.

5. _____ Committed lovers have fun together and are unlikely to share tedious times.

6. _____ People usually confine themselves to one particular love style.

7. _____ Arranged marriages are often examples of pragma.

8. _____ In real life, a relationship usually focuses on one of John Lee's "love styles."

9. _____ Martyrs usually have good intentions; they believe that loving involves doing unselfishly for others without voicing their own needs in return.

10. _____ Manipulating and martyring are both sometimes mistaken for love.

11. _____ People with very high self-esteem often experience a persistent and insatiable need for affection.

12. _____ M-frame relationships rest on interdependence.

13. _____ Loving is a product that is found.

14. _____ For most people, falling in love produces anxiety.

15. _____ Lovers don't automatically live happily ever after.

SHORT ANSWER

1. The text points out that love may satisfy *legitimate* and *illegitimate* needs. List two in each category and briefly discuss their importance.

2.   How does *consummate love* fit into the triangular theory of love?

3.   Sometimes lovers say they would be willing to "do anything" for the sake of their beloved. Is this the same thing as "martyring?" Why or why not?

4.   In Reiss's Wheel Theory of Love, why does the rapport stage precede the self-revelation stage? Explain in terms of process.

5.   What is the difference between self-love and narcissism?

ESSAY

1. Explain what love is and what it is not.

2. In what way(s) is self-worth (self-esteem) a prerequisite to love or loving? That is, does self-worth seem to be required before one can fully love?

3. Compare and contrast Sternberg's Triangular Theory of Love with Reiss's Wheel Theory of Love. Do they have similar goals? Do they address similar or different issues?

4. Explain John Lee's six contemporary love styles. Provide at least one illustration of each.

5. The text describes love as a *discovery*, rather than something that is "found." Explain this point of view and give an example to support your answer.

Chapter 5

ANSWERS TO SAMPLE QUESTIONS

Completion (using key terms)

1.	emotion	14.	symbiotic relationship
2.	Legitimate needs	15.	Self-esteem
3.	Illegitimate needs	16.	Narcissism
4.	consummate love	17.	dependence
5.	Love styles	18.	rapport
6.	eros	19.	Independence
7.	storge	20.	interdependent
8.	pragma	21.	H-frame
9.	agape	22.	M-frame
10.	ludus	23.	wheel of love
11.	mania	24.	Mutuality
12.	Martyring	25.	Being realistic
13.	Manipulating	26.	Co-dependent

Multiple Choice (page references in parentheses)

1.	b (102)	19.	a (113)
2.	a (103)	20.	b (112)
3.	c (104)	21.	a (113)
4.	b (104)	22.	d (114)
5.	d (105)	23.	a (114)
6.	a (106)	24.	b (114)
7.	b (105)	25.	c (116)
8.	d (106)	26.	c (105)
9.	d (107)	27.	b (109)
10.	a (107)	28.	c (109)
11.	c (108)	29.	b (110)
12.	b (108)	30.	b (110)
13.	a (108)	31.	c (113)
14.	d (108)	32.	c (113)
15.	c (108)	33.	c (116)
16.	a (110)	34.	c (105)
17.	c (111)	35.	d (106)
18.	d (111)		

True-False (page references in parentheses)

1.	T (102)	9.	T (109)
2.	F (103)	10.	T (111)
3.	T (103)	11.	F (113)
4.	T (104)	12.	T (114)
5.	F (105)	13.	F (114)
6.	F (107)	14.	T (114)
7.	T (108)	15.	T (116)
8.	F (108)		

CHAPTER 6

OUR SEXUAL SELVES

CHAPTER SUMMARY

From childhood to old age, people are sexual beings. Knowledge about children's sexual development and the emergence of sexual orientation is sketchy to begin with and, furthermore, not agreed upon by experts. We do know that humans development into sexually expressive beings beginning in childhood. As we develop into sexually expressive individuals, we manifest a **sexual orientation**, referring to whether we are **heterosexual**, **homosexual**, or **bisexual**. From the interactionist point of view, the previous concepts are social inventions. It has been a point of disagreement about who is to be categorized as **gay** or **lesbian**. The origins of both heterosexual and gay identities remain a puzzle. Virtually all the studies of child sexual development have methodological limitations.

There are various theoretical perspectives concerning human sexuality. From the **interpersonal exchange model of sexual satisfaction**, satisfaction depends on the costs and rewards of a sexual relationship. The **interactionist theoretical perspective on human sexuality** holds that women and men are influenced by **sexual scripts**.Whatever one's sexual orientation, sexual expression is negotiated with cultural messages about what is sexually permissible, even desirable. In the United States, the cultural messages have moved from one that encouraged **patriarchal sex** and reproduction as its principal purpose, to a message that encourages **expressive sexuality** in myriad ways for both genders equally. During the 1980s and 1990s, there have been a number of challenges to **heterosexism**, although **homophobia** is still present in American society. While pleasure seeking was the icon of sixties sexuality, caution in the face of risk characterizes contemporary times.

Sociologist Ira Reiss has formulated four standards of nonmarital sex: abstinence, permissiveness with affection, permissiveness without affection, and the double standard. There are differences among racial/ethnic groups in sexual expression. African Americans may be more sexually expressive and less inhibited than other Americans.

Marital sex changes throughout life. Young spouses tend to place greater emphasis on sex than do older mates. But, while the frequency of sexual intercourse declines over time and the length of a marriage, a NORC survey indicates that the average frequency of sex for sexually active, married respondents under age sixty was seven times a month. On average, as people get older, they have sex less often. As people age, they point to the total marital relationship rather than just to intercourse. Some older partners shift from intercourse to petting as a preferred sexual activity. Boredom can affect marital sex. Despite declining sexual frequency, sexual satisfaction remains high in marriages over the life course.

Making sex a **pleasure bond**, whether married or not, involves cooperating in a nurturing, caring relationship. To fully cooperate sexually, partners need to assume **sexual responsibility**, to break free from restrictive gendered stereotypes, and to communicate openly. Research shows a correlation between sexual satisfaction and self-esteem. High self-esteem allows us to engage in **pleasuring**. A second element in making sex a pleasure bond is the ability to transcend gender stereotypes. A third element is communication and cooperation. A very important ingredient in sexual sharing is a **holistic view of sex**. It is important for partners to make the time for intimacy.

HIV/AIDS has now been known for twenty-five years. Not including AIDS, more than 65 million Americans currently live with **sexually transmitted diseases (STDs)**. Primary risk groups for AIDS are men who have sex with men. The disease has affected young and middle-aged adults the most. HIV/AIDS affects heterosexuals as well as gay men. The burdens of AIDS are not all emotional, nor do they always involve physical care of victims; some are financial. Children are also affected by AIDS.

Political and religious conflict over sexuality characterized the 1980s and 1990s. Conservatives use political processes, including lobbying, campaign contributions, and getting out the vote to try to shape public policy on sex matters. Many controversies still rage over sex education. Abstinence-only education has yet to prove effective.

People today are making decisions about sex in a climate characterized by political conflict over sexual issues. In such a climate, making knowledgeable choices is a must.

LEARNING OBJECTIVES

Based on your careful and thorough reading of Chapter 6, you should:

1.   be familiar with the processes involved in children's sexual development and the dynamics of sexual orientation.

2.   understand the key theoretical perspectives on human sexuality.

3.   be familiar with Reiss's four standards of nonmarital sex and the racial-ethnic differences in terms of sexual expression.

4.   be familiar with the sexually-related changes that take place throughout marriage.

5.   understand the concept of sex as a pleasure bond and the importance of communication, cooperation, and sharing in sexual relationships.

6.   be familiar with the sexually transmitted diseases that are discussed in the text, including HIV/AIDS.

7.   be acquainted with the relationship between religion and politics as they relate to sexuality and the politics of sex education.

8.   understand the concept of sexual responsibility.

KEY TERMS (page references in parentheses)

abstinence (131)
asexual (119)
asexuality (123)
bisexual (119)
double standard (132)
expressive sexuality (127)
friends with benefits (132
gay (124)
GLBT (124)
habituation (138)

habituation hypothesis (134)
heterosexism (128)
heterosexual (123)
HIV/AIDS (146)
holistic view of sex (141)
homophobia (129)
homosexual (123)
interactionist perspective on sexuality (126)
interpersonal exchange model of sexual
        satisfaction (125)

lesbian (124)
patriarchal sexuality (126)
permissiveness with affection (131)
permissiveness without affection (131)
pleasure bond (140)
pleasuring (141)

sexual orientation (123)
sexual responsibility (140)
sexual scripts (126)
sexually transmitted diseases (STDs) (142)
spectatoring (141)

COMPLETION (using key terms)

1.	The terms *heterosexuality* and *homosexuality* relate to a person's _____.

2.	A homosexual male is referred to as a _____ male.

3.	A homosexual female is referred to as a _____.

4.	_____ refers to a fear of homosexuality.

5.	The standard of _____ permits nonmarital intercourse for both men and women equally, provided they have a fairly stable affectionate relationship.

6.	Sometimes called recreational sex, the standard of _____ allows intercourse for women and men regardless of how much stability or affection is in their relationship.

7.	A(n) _____ view of sex sees sex as an extension of the whole relationship rather than as a purely physical exchange.

8.	Masters, Johnson, and Kolodny believe that sex is a(n) _____ by which partners commit themselves to expressing their sexual feelings with each other.

9.	Not including AIDS, more than 65 million Americans currently live with _____ diseases.

10.	The standard of _____ maintains that regardless of the circumstances, nonmarital intercourse is wrong for both women and men.

KEY THEORETICAL PERSPECTIVES

interpersonal exchange model of sexual satisfaction
interactionist perspective on human sexuality
Reiss's standards of nonmarital sex

Chapter 6

INTERNET AND INFOTRAC EXERCISES

Internet Exercises

1. Note that the "sexual satisfaction quiz" involved in this exercise is not necessarily scientific, but may be thought-provoking nevertheless. Go to: http://quiz.ivillage.co.uk/uk_relationships/tests/sexsat.htm. Take the quiz. Respond to the following questions:
    * Do you agree with the interpretation based on your responses to the quiz? Why or why not?
    * Do you think sexual satisfaction can be measured? Why or why not?

2. Since the initial appearance of the drug Viagra, which is designed to deal with erectile dysfunction in men, a variety of other similar products have appeared, with some available only by prescription (e.g., Cialis, Levitra), while others are available through mail order and without a prescription (e.g., Enzyte). Visit the websites for each of these products:

    http://www.viagra.com/index.asp

    http://www.cialis.com/index.jsp?reqNavId=0?ccd=cise600

    http://www.levitra.com/

    http://enzite.net/

    After you have browsed these sites, respond to the following questions:
    * Various products appear to have dealt rather effectively with many men's problems with impotency. What are your feelings on this issue? If you are male and if you were (or are) having this kind of difficulty, would you consider taking one of these products? Why or why not?
    * Thus far, no equally successful drug has been developed/approved for use by women who are experiencing sexual dysfunction. Does this surprise you? Why or why not?

3. AIDS.org is a website devoted to educating the public about this disease. Go to: http://www.aids.org/FactSheets/. There you will find a wealth of information about HIV/AIDS. Try clicking on "Facts About AIDS," "Stopping the Spread of AIDS," "Safer Sex Guidelines," and "Drug Use and HIV Prevention." After you have read the contents of each, respond to the following questions:
    * Did you learn anything you did not already know? If so, what?
    * If you are sexually active with more than one sexual partner, do you practice "safe sex?" How?
    * Do you think the threat of HIV/AIDS provides additional motivation to have only one sex partner, including within the realm of marriage?
    * Short of finding a preventive vaccination for HIV/AIDS, do you think the incidence of this disease will increase or decline in the future? Why?

4. GLBT is the acronym for gay, lesbian, bisexual and transgender individuals. At www.glbt.org you will find a website that provides a variety of support mechanisms and a host of information. Read about some of the resources and networks. Did you know that there were so many resources available for those who are gay, lesbian, bisexual or transgender?

InfoTrac Exercises

1.   Use the key phrase *AIDS/HIV*. Examine a few of the many articles that will be generated by this search, then respond to the following questions:
  • How do American attitudes toward AIDS/HIV today compare with attitudes when this disease first appeared on the scene in the early 1980s?
  • What are your reactions to the fact that wealthy persons are able to afford the drugs that can effectively "slow" the progress of the AIDS virus, but less fortunate Americans are left at the mercy of the disease?
  • Do you think that medical science will find an effective cure for AIDS? What is the basis for your prediction?

2.   Use the key words *sexual behavior surveys; evaluation*. From the articles listed, browse through the titles and focus on those that deal with *actual research* on human sexual behavior. Read these articles. Respond to the following questions:
  • What are the key limitations of surveys involving sexual behavior? Do you think that people can be expected to be honest in this kind of survey situation? Why or why not?
  • In view of life threatening diseases like AIDS, do you think our government should sponsor a nationwide survey concerning Americans' sexual behavior? What political obstacles do you think might be encountered if such an effort was mounted?
  • Do you think we will ever be able to obtain completely accurate information about Americans' sexual behavior? Why or why not?

3.   Use the key words *sex education for children*. Focus on the articles that deal with "abstinence only" sex education strategies. Read these articles. Respond to the following questions:
  • Do you think that "abstinence only" sex education programs are effective? Why or why not?
  • Provided you approve of sex education in our schools, when do you think it should begin? If you are opposed to sex education in our schools, what are your suggestions for how young people should acquire accurate answers to their questions about sexuality?
  • If a young person under age 18 has decided to become sexually active, should he/she be able to obtain reliable birth control devices? Why or why not?

4.   Use the key words *homosexuality; television*. Select two or three articles that deal with "homosexual characters in television programs." It should be obvious that homosexuality is a fairly common topic within prime-time television programming. Respond to the following questions:
  • Do you think that homosexuality on television poses a threat to our society? Why or why not?
  • If you were a social policy maker, what approach would you take toward homosexuality in the media? Should there be any restrictions? If so, what?
  • Do you think that as a topic on television, homosexuality will become so common as to almost go unnoticed? Why or why not?

MULTIPLE CHOICE

1. _____ The text points out that we tend to think of sexual orientation as a
   a. continuum.
   b. dichotomy.
   c. product.
   d. process.

2. _____ Which of the following does NOT relate to sexual orientation?
   a. transsexual
   b. homosexual
   c. heterosexual
   d. bisexual

3. _____ In evaluating sexual satisfaction, suppose that an individual evaluates what options are available and how good these options are in comparison with his/her present relationship. This reflects which theoretical perspective?
   a. structure-functional
   b. biosocial
   c. interpersonal exchange model
   d. interactionist

4. _____ "Sex has different cultural meanings and plays a different role in different social settings. In the United States (and elsewhere), messages about sex have changed over time." These statements illustrate which theoretical perspective?
   a. structure-functional
   b. biosocial
   c. interpersonal exchange model
   d. interactionist

5. _____ The U.S. Supreme Court decision in *Griswold v. Connecticut* (1965)
   a. extended the concept of "privacy" to single individuals.
   b. stated a right of "marital privacy" – the idea that sexual and reproductive decision making belongs to the couple, not to the state.
   c. extended the concept of "privacy" to minors.
   d. denied the right of "marital privacy."

6. _____ The text points out that recently the American public's attitudes toward homosexuality have
   a. not changed from the previous three decades.
   b. become even more unfavorable.
   c. become more favorable.
   d. continued to fluctuate.

7. _____ Which of the following is a fear, dread, aversion or hatred of homosexuality?
   a. gayphobia
   b. homosensitization
   c. homophobia
   d. GLBTphobia

8. _____ In a large national sample of 12,000 volunteers from the Seattle, San Francisco, and Washington, DC areas, sociologists Philip Blumstein and Pepper Schwartz compared four types of couples. Which of the following is NOT one of these groups?
   a.   heterosexual marrieds
   b.   cohabiting heterosexuals
   c.   gay males
   d.   cohabiting bisexuals

9. _____ Another term for "abstinence" is
   a.   virginity.
   b.   celibacy.
   c.   permissiveness.
   d.   *coitus interruptus.*

10. _____ Sexual intercourse between partners only briefly acquainted, which is also referred to as "casual sex," reflects
   a.   the double standard.
   b.   permissiveness with affection.
   c.   abstinence.
   d.   permissiveness without affection.

11. _____ David and Lucy are siblings in their teens. Their parents advocate sexual abstinence for Lucy, but do not discipline David for premarital sexual activity. This situation illustrates
   a.   permissiveness with affection.
   b.   celibacy.
   c.   the double standard.
   d.   archaic sexual expression.

12. _____ Like heterosexual behavior, gay/lesbian sexuality has been explored among African Americans mostly in the context of
   a.   sexual freedom.
   b.   problems.
   c.   liberation.
   d.   androgyny.

13. _____ The average number of times that married persons under age 25 have sex is about _____ times a month.
   a.   2
   b.   4
   c.   8
   d.   12

14. _____ According to the text, the high frequency of intercourse among young married partners may reflect
   a.   genetic differences.
   b.   hormonal changes.
   c.   a self-fulfilling prophecy.
   d.   biosocial theory.

15. _____ The text observes that the convergence of sexual satisfaction with general satisfaction serves to support Masters, Johnson, and Kolodny's view that sex is a
   a.   pleasure bond.
   b.   responsibility.
   c.   partnership.
   d.   cooperative agreement.

16. _____ According to the text, high self-esteem is important to pleasurable sex because it
   a.   allows individuals to acknowledge and accept their own tastes and preferences.
   b.   provides the freedom to search for new pleasures.
   c.   allows people to engage in pleasuring.
   d.   all of the above

17. _____ Consider this statement: "My husband and I are first of all a man and a woman–sexual creatures all through. That's where we get our real and central life satisfactions. If that's not right, nothing is." This point of view reflects what the text refers to as
   a.   sexual sharing.
   b.   a holistic view of sex.
   c.   intimacy.
   d.   open communication.

18. _____ Which of the following groups currently has the highest number of active cases of HIV/AIDS?
   a.   Asian Pacific Islanders
   b.   American Indians
   c.   Hispanics
   d.   Non-Hispanic Blacks

19. _____ Currently, _____ people in the United States are infected with HIV.
   a.   450,000
   b.   650,000
   c.   750,000
   d.   850,000

20. _____ The text addresses four principles of sexual responsibility that may serve as guidelines for sexual decision making. Which of the following is NOT one of these?
   a.   the possibility of pregnancy
   b.   the possibility of contracting sexual transmitted diseases or transmitting them to someone else
   c.   the possibility of emotional harm to one's sexual partner
   d.   communicating with partners or potential sexual partners

21. _____ Sex education programs that are defined as "abstinence plus" include which of the following?
   a.   no information about contraception
   b.   no information about AIDS
   c.   information about contraception and AIDS
   d.   a brief introduction to methods of contraception

22. _____ Research by Frank Furstenberg has a revealed which of the following about adolescent sexuality?
    a.   sexual activity has dramatically declined
    b.   sexual activity has slowed
    c.   sexual activity has increased
    d.   rates of oral sex have declined

23. _____ According to Masters, Johnson and Kolodny, it is critical that couples
    a.   have intercourse on a regular basis.
    b.   communicate with one another.
    c.   not lose touch with their sexuality and their ability to share it.
    d.   not worry about lack of desire that accompanies old age.

24. _____ Which of the following is NOT a principle for sexual sharing?
    a.   having an attitude of mutuality
    b.   judging each others needs
    c.   deepening a holistic view of sex
    d.   maintaining a holistic view of sex

25. _____ Which term is used by Masters and Johnson to define the processes of emotionally removing oneself from a sexual encounter?
    a.   pleasuring
    b.   bonding
    c.   spectatoring
    d.   communicating

26. _____ Habituation is used to describe which of the following?
    a.   the lack of sexual contact among older married couples
    b.   decreased interest due to increased accessibility
    c.   a lack of change in the frequency
    d.   increase in marital sexual frequency

27. _____ Which of the following is least likely to be an effect of extramarital affairs?
    a.   exposure to various sexually transmitted diseases
    b.   financial exploitation
    c.   divorce
    d.   regaining trust

28. _____ What term is used to describe the marital infidelity that involves the Internet?
    a.   net sex
    b.   online sex
    c.   super sex
    d.   cyberadultery

29. _____ Which of the following is NOT considered a risk factor for extramarital sex?
   a. opportunity
   b. strong sex interest
   c. permissive sexual values
   d. habituation

30. _____ All of the following are recent studies of sexuality in the United States EXCEPT
   a. National Opinion Research Center.
   b. University of Wisconsin National Survey of Families and Households.
   c. Indiana University Kinsey Research Project.
   d. National Opinion Research Center.

TRUE-FALSE

1. _____ Children are maturing physically later than in the past.

2. _____ Virtually all the studies of child sexual development, including those attempting to determine the origin of sexual orientation, have methodological limitations.

3. _____ A 1992 NORC survey found that men were considerably more likely than women to perform or "do," sex.

4. _____ In recent years, sexual activity has declined among youth, and that is especially true for black youth.

5. _____ Most unmarried young adults engage in sexual relations, and there are more of them today than in the past due to delayed marriage.

6. _____ According to the double standard, women's sexual behavior must be more conservative than men's.

7. _____ Being "respectable" is unimportant to both adult and teen African American women.

8. _____ According to Pepper Schwartz, "people don't have sex every week; they have good weeks and bad weeks."

9. _____ Declining sexual frequency throughout most marriages leads to lowered levels of sexual satisfaction and this dissatisfaction increases over the life course.

10. _____ Most children with AIDS contracted it from their mothers during pregnancy, at birth, or through breast milk.

SHORT ANSWER

1.   Define *sexual orientation*. What is the difference between *heterosexual, homosexual,* and *bisexual*?

2.   Describe the relationship between increased age and sexual behavior.

3.   How can HIV/AIDS be transmitted from one person to another?

4.   Explain what is meant by the "double standard." Provide an example.

5.   List and briefly explain Troiden's four stages of homosexual identity formation.

ESSAY

1.   Explain how sexual response is related to self-esteem, pleasure, communication, and sharing.

2.   Describe sexuality through the various stages of marriage. Be sure to use specific concepts and research results where appropriate.

3.   Is there a need for society - or its agents-to structure or in other ways shape the human sexual response? If yes, why? If no, why not?

4.   How are politics and sex education related? Give several illustrations.

5.   Discuss the various ways in which HIV/AIDS has affected families.

ANSWERS TO SAMPLE QUESTIONS

Completion (key terms)

1.	sexual orientation	6.	permissiveness without affection
2.	gay	7.	holistic
3.	lesbian	8.	pleasure bond
4.	Homophobia	9.	sexually transmitted
5.	permissiveness with affection	10.	abstinence

Multiple Choice (page references in parentheses)

1.	b (123)	16.	d (140)
2.	a (123)	17.	b (141)
3.	c (125)	18.	d (145)
4.	d (125)	19.	d (144)
5.	b (128)	20.	c (144)
6.	c (128)	21.	c (147)
7.	c (129)	22.	b (146)
8.	d (129)	23.	b (138)
9.	b (131)	24.	b (141-142)
10.	d (131)	25.	c (141)
11.	c (132)	26.	b (138)
12.	b (140)	27.	d (135)
13.	d (137)	28.	d (134)
14.	c (137)	29.	d (134)
15.	a (140)	30.	c (136)

True-False (page references in parentheses)

1.	F (122)	6.	T (132)
2.	T (125)	7.	F (139)
3.	T (124)	8.	T (136)
4.	T (128)	9.	F (139)
5.	T (128)	10.	T (143)

CHAPTER 7

Marriage: From Social Institution to Private Relationship

CHAPTER SUMMARY

That marriages should involve romance and lead to personal satisfaction is a uniquely modern – and Western – idea. The marriage picture is changing as is indicated by changing birth, divorce and marriage rates. Today, fewer than two-thirds of adults in the United States are married.

Marriage marked the joining of two individuals as well as their kinship groups. The time-honored premises of marriage were the **expectation of permanence** and the **expectation of sexual exclusivity**. Now **polygamy** is culturally accepted in parts of the world, and in other places the social arrangement of **swinging** is practiced. Marriages have transitioned from **communal** to **individualistic** where one's own interests are a valid concern. This has resulted in the authority of kin and extended family being weakened. Individuals have begun finding their own marriage partners, and romantic love is now considered a part of marriage. The kinship of married people is made up of their **family of orientation** as well as their **family of procreation**. Unlike many cultures, the American housing architecture discourages families from living in extended family households.

Arranged marriages that were used to consolidate family property were replaced by marriages that were based on the ideology of romantic love. Marriage reached a point where time-honored traditions were much less important than in the past. **Companionate** marriages then replaced institutional marriages. Marriage became an opportunity to have a single family home with a white picket fence. However, as women entered the work force and gained an education, the orientation moved from a **companionate** to an **individualistic** orientation. Individualized marriages have much more flexible roles for both spouses and the marriage involves love, communication and emotional intimacy.

Today, marriages have taken a variety of forms where tolerance and diversity are more common and many observers refer to this as the **deinstitutionalization** of marriage. In today's marriages, spouses have had greater wealth and assets, earned higher wages, had more frequent and better sex, and overall better health among other quality of life issues. Today's children have not fared as well in the families created by marriage. Children fared much better in married families as opposed to one-parent families. Children were less likely to drop out of high school; they had more contact with parents, and were less likely to live in poverty.

Some conservative Christian organizations are proposing covenant marriage in which partners agree to be bound by a marriage covenant, stronger than the ordinary contract. The **Healthy Marriage Initiative** encourages marriage education programs in an effort to promote healthy families. The **Temporary Assistance for Needy Families** "welfare reform" program also has family-related goals designed to reduce the number of out-of-wedlock pregnancies and encourage the number of two-parent families. Marriage offers individuals the experience of building a relationship over time and provides individuals with a sense of obligation to others as well as the larger community.

Chapter 7

LEARNING OBJECTIVES

Based on your careful and thorough reading of Chapter 7, you should:

1.   understand the major indicators of marital status – marriage, divorce and birth rates.

2.   be familiar with the terms *expectation of permanence* and *expectation of sexual exclusivity*.

3.   understand the subcultures of polygamy, polyamory and swinging.

4.   be familiar with the changing premises of marriage.

5.   understand the terms *family of orientation* and *family of procreation*.

6.   know the meaning of courtly love.

7.   understand the similarities and differences between companionate marriage and individualized marriage.

8.   understand the consequences of the changing marriage patterns as they relate to children.

9.   be familiar with the family decline perspective.

10.   understand the Healthy Marriage Initiative, its purposes and its criticisms.

11.   know about the family change perspective.

12.   understand how marriage, happiness, and life satisfaction are related

KEY TERMS (page references in parentheses)

collectivist society (160)
communal society (160)
companionate marriage (165)
courtly love (163)
covenant marriage (173)
deinstitutionalization of marriage (164)
expectations of permanence (158)
expectations of sexual exclusivity (158)
experience hypothesis (169)
extended family (160)
family of orientation (161)
family of procreation (163)
Healthy Marriage Initiative (HMI) (174)
individualism (160)
individualistic society (160)

individualized marriage (166)
kin (160)
la familia (161)
marriage premise (165)
pluralistic family (168)
polyamory (159)
polyandry (158)
polygamy (158)
polygyny (158)
selection hypothesis (169)
social institution (158)
swinging (159)
Temporary Assistance for Needy Families (TANF) (174)

COMPLETION (using key terms)

1. A family characterized by tolerance and diversity is a _____ family.

2. In the United States, couples enter into marriage with the expectation of _____ and the expectation of _____.

3. _____ means being married to more than one spouse.

4. The family of _____ is the one into which you are born.

5. Having more than one husband is _____.

6. An _____ family includes parents and other relatives.

7. A _____ marriage is one in which partners agree to be bound by a marriage covenant.

8. A marriage arrangement in which couples exchange partners in order to engage in recreational sex is called _____.

9. The extended as well as the nuclear family make up what is known as _____.

10. An optional marriage between spouses with flexible roles is an _____ marriage.

INTERNET AND INFOTRAC EXERCISES

Internet Exercises

1. At Michael Kearl's website http://www.trinity.edu/~mkearl/fam-type.html#cu you will find a page on the Structure of Contemporary Families and Households

    After reading the main content of the page, click on the links to other information on the family.
    - How have marriage changed in the last 20 years, 30 years in form?
    - Do you think that families are in better shape or not?

2. Go to http://marriage.families.com/blog/defining-marriage-what-about-polygamy in order to learn more about polygamy. After reading "Defining Marriage: What about Polygamy?" answer the following questions:
    - Do you think you could live in a polygamous relationship?
    - Do you think that Warren Jeff's polygamous marriages were fair to the women?

3. Cohabitation is one alternative to marriage discussed in the text. There is a website that focuses exclusively on different alternatives to marriage, and may be found at http://www.unmarried.org After you reach the main page, click on "Facts and Fun." If you have time, you may wish to explore other features of this site. Following your review of the contents of this website, respond to the following questions:
    - The text discusses the relationship between cohabitation and the likelihood of marriage and between cohabitation and marital quality. Of course, another alternative is choosing not to marry *or* to cohabit with another person. What are your personal feelings about the different alternatives to marriage?
    - Would you consider remaining single for the rest of your life, or, if you are married, but were to divorce, would you consider a permanent single lifestyle? Why or why not?

4. To learn more about the Healthy Marriage Initiative, go to http://www.acf.hhs.gov/healthymarriage/about/mission.html and read about the program and what it hopes to accomplish.
   - Do you think that this initiative will accomplish its goals?
   - Of all the goals stated, which ones do you think are beneficial for the couples and children?

InfoTrac Exercises

1. Use the key phrase *autobiography of an arranged marriage*. Then, access the article entitled, "Autobiography of an Arranged Marriage: An African American Woman's Love Story." Read the article. Respond to the following questions:
   - Presumably, the woman in this account had previously experienced marriage by her own "free choice." Later in her life, she opted for an arranged marriage. Based on your reading of her story, why do you think she did this?
   - Would you consider an arranged marriage? Why or why not?

2. Use the key phrase *sex and the marriage market*. This will produce an article by James Q. Wilson in which the author discusses the impact of the marriage market on women in the United States. Wilson observes that there are more marriageable women than there are men, and discusses the implications of this fact in American society. After you have read the article, respond to the following questions:
   - Within your circle of friends and acquaintances, focus on women who are unmarried. Are these people single *voluntarily*, or are they interested in marriage, but have not found a suitable partner? If they are experiencing difficulty, do you think this predicament has anything to do with the *marriage market*? Why or why not?

3. Use the keyword *interracial marriage*. From the list of articles, select those that focus on the increasing phenomenon of interracial marriage in American society (There should be articles from magazines like *Newsweek* and *Time*). After you have read these articles, respond to the following questions:
   - Would you seriously consider an interracial/interethnic marriage? Why or why not?
   - Do you think there will ever be a time in American society when interracial/interethnic marriage is NOT regarded as "unusual?"

TRUE-FALSE

1. _____ The marriage and divorce rates are indicators of the changing picture of marriage.

2. _____ There is an increasing tendency for individuals to marry in their early 20s.

3. _____ Polyandry means many marriages.

4. _____ Swinging allows partners to exchange partners for recreational sex.

5. _____ The family of procreation is formed by marriage and having children.

6. _____   An institutional marriage is based on the norm of permanence.

7. _____   Pluralistic marriages were found in the 1920s.

8. _____   Covenant marriage is a practice that has been in existence for hundreds of years.

9. _____   Individualized marriages are considered optional.

10. _____   Americans value marriage and would like to marry, but for many of them marriage is a goal that is difficult to achieve.

MULTIPLE CHOICE

1. _____   The marriage rate in the United States has _____ since 1950.
   a.   slightly increased
   b.   generally declined
   c.   remained the same
   d.   dramatically increased

2. _____   There are several rates that are considered indicators of the marriage picture. Which of the following is not one of those indicators?
   a.   birth
   b.   divorce
   c.   death
   d.   remarriage

3. _____   A result of the increase in divorce is that
   a.   there is a decrease in eligible partners.
   b.   more people are postponing marriage.
   c.   there in an increase in the number of singles.
   d.   remarriage for widows is impossible.

4. _____   The practice of having more than one spouse is known as
   a.   polygamy.
   b.   polyandry.
   c.   polyamory.
   d.   polygyny.

5. _____   Having many lovers or having the option to love others in addition to their spouses is
   a.   polyandry.
   b.   polyamory.
   c.   polygyny.
   d.   polygamy.

6. _____   When couples exchange partners to engage in recreational sex, they are said to be
   a.   semi-adulterous.
   b.   mate swapping.
   c.   partying.
   d.   swinging.

7. _____ An individualistic orientation towards marriage has resulted in all of the following EXCEPT
   a. the authority of kin has been strengthened.
   b. individuals have begun to find their own partners.
   c. romantic love has become associated with marriage.
   d. the extended family is less important.

8. _____ The family that is formed by marrying and having children is the
   a. family of orientation.
   b. extended family.
   c. family of procreation.
   d. fictive kin family.

9. _____ Companionate marriage, as defined by Burgess, was characterized by all of the following EXCEPT
   a. sharp division of labor.
   b. emotional satisfaction.
   c. single earner in the household.
   d. expectations for self-actualization for the wife.

10. _____ An individualized marriage is one that
    a. involves love and communication.
    b. involves unequal decision making.
    c. requires an unfair division of household labor.
    d. focuses on outward appearances.

11. _____ A family that is characterized by tolerance and diversity is a(n)
    a. individualistic family.
    b. pluralistic family.
    c. communal family.
    d. companionate family.

12. _____ In Waite's examination of married and unmarried households, she reported that spouses in married households had all of the following EXCEPT
    a. overall better health.
    b. earned higher wages.
    c. had higher rates of alcohol use.
    d. had an orderly lifestyle.

13. _____ Children raised in married families were
    a. more likely to live in poverty.
    b. more likely to drop out of school.
    c. more likely to be in trouble at school.
    d. had more contact with parents.

14. _____ Ahmed concludes that arranged marriage performs certain functions. Which of the following is NOT one of these?
    a. maintains sexual fidelity
    b. affirms and strengthens parents' power over their children
    c. enhances the value of the kinship group
    d. helps keep the family traditions and value systems intact

15. _____ The proportion of children under age fifteen living with two married parents has
    a.   increased dramatically.
    b.   remained the same as in the 70s.
    c.   increased slightly.
    d.   declined.

16. _____ The hypothesis that many of the benefits associated with marriage are due to the personal characteristics of those who choose to marry is the
    a.   health selection hypothesis.
    b.   experience hypothesis.
    c.   mate connection hypothesis.
    d.   selection hypothesis.

17. _____ An African American tradition that is being revived at weddings is
    a.   feeding each other cake.
    b.   jumping the broom.
    c.   toasting with African wines.
    d.   carrying the bride across the threshold.

18. _____ A relatively new type of marriage in which couples agree to be bound by agreement stronger than a contract is a
    a.   prenuptial agreement marriage.
    b.   contractual marriage.
    c.   marriage solemnization.
    d.   covenant marriage.

19. _____ Which of the following is a program that promotes marriage education?
    a.   Temporary Assistance for Needy Families
    b.   Marriage Reform Assistance
    c.   Healthy Marriage Initiative
    d.   Parents And Children Together

20. _____ The Temporary Assistance for Needy Families has as its goals all of the following EXCEPT
    a.   end the dependence of needy parents.
    b.   reduce incidence of out-of-wedlock pregnancies.
    c.   encourage formation of two-parent households.
    d.   teach single mothers how to remain independent.

21. _____ Which of the following is not a traditional family function handed down from Roman Catholic Canon Law?
    a.   guaranteeing property rights
    b.   providing economically for family members
    c.   assuring children will not be born out-of-wedlock
    d.   bringing the children up responsibly

22. _____ Laws in the United States require that all marriages are
    a.   cenogamous.
    b.   monogamous.
    c.   polyamorous.
    d.   polyandrous.

23. _____   What term is used to describe friends that are so close that they are like relatives?
      a.   kissing cousins
      b.   semi-cousins
      c.   fictional family
      d.   fictive kin

24. _____   Talcott Parsons described kinship in the United States as
      a.   procreation - orientation relationships.
      b.   multi-layered kinship groups.
      c.   interlocking conjugal families.
      d.   hyper-extended families.

25. _____   Which of the following programs was designed as a welfare reform program?
      a.   Healthy Marriage Initiative
      b.   No Child Left Behind
      c.   Temporary Assistance for Needy Families
      d.   Planned Parenthood

26. _____   Which of the following hypotheses states that just the experience of being married creates the same benefits as the selection hypothesis?
      a.   marriage hypothesis
      b.   transition hypothesis
      c.   selection hypothesis
      d.   monogamy hypothesis

27. _____   The proportion of children living with two parents in the United States has declined from 85 percent in 1970 to _____ percent in 2005.
      a.   78
      b.   67
      c   56
      d.   45

28. _____   Which of the following terms has been used to describe an institutional marriage bond?
      a.   coupled
      b.   yoked
      c.   patriarchal
      d.   matriarchal

29. _____   Federal policy in the War on Poverty did which of the following to decrease poverty?
      a.   encouraged individual responsibility
      b.   offered structural strategies
      c.   raised welfare benefits
      d.   increased income tax

30. _____   All of the following are characteristics of children growing up in poverty EXCEPT
      a.   they live in environmentally unhealthy neighborhoods.
      b.   they do not have nutritious meals.
      c.   have more behavioral problems.
      d.   have fewer health problems.

TRUE-FALSE

1. _____ The marriage and divorce rates are indicators of the changing picture of marriage.

2. _____ There is an increasing tendency for individuals to marry in their early 20s.

3. _____ Polyandry means many marriages.

4. _____ Swinging allows partners to exchange partners for recreational sex.

5. _____ The family of procreation is formed by marriage and having children.

6. _____ An institutional marriage is based on the norm of permanence.

7. _____ Pluralistic marriages were found in the 1920s.

8. _____ Covenant marriage is a practice that has been in existence for hundreds of years.

9. _____ Individualized marriages are considered optional.

10. _____ Americans value marriage and would like to marry, but for many of them marriage is a goal that is difficult to achieve.

SHORT ANSWER

1. What is the difference between arranged marriage and companionate marriage? Give an example of each.

2.   Define *polygamy* and *polyamory*. Give an example of each.

3.   What is the difference between "marriage" and "covenant marriage?" What explains this change?

4.   What does "deinstitutionalization of marriage" mean? Give an example.

5.   Who are fictive kin and who are extended family members? How do they differ?

ESSAY

1.   Explore the extent to which mate selection is a "bargaining" relationship. Support your answer with pertinent data and research findings.

2.   Jeff married Sharon. Sharon and Jeff are both white and Roman Catholic. They met at a private, liberal arts college with a predominantly white, middle- and upper-middle class student population. Jeff majored in sociology and Sharon was majoring in psychology. They met and became acquainted while taking classes in the same academic building. What sociological concepts, factors, and/or theories help us to understand how this could have happened?

3.   Discuss the issue of polygamous marriages. What are some of the problems that these relationships encounter, how does society view them, and who is most likely to participate?

4.   Imagine that your friend has confided in you that he/she is planning a covenant marriage and, since you are in a family sociology class, wants to know "the facts" about the ceremony and especially about the probability of eventual marriage and happiness in marriage.

5.   What does the transition from "yoke mates" to "soul mates" mean? Give examples of both.

ANSWERS TO SAMPLE QUESTIONS

Completion (using key terms)

1.   pluralistic
2.   permanence, sexual exclusivity
3.   Polygamy
4.   orientation
5.   polyandry

6.   extended
7.   covenant
8.   swinging
9.   *la familia*
10. individualsitic

Multiple Choice (page references in parentheses)

1.   b (155)
2.   d (155)
3.   c (156)
4.   a (158)
5.   b (159)
6.   b (159)
7.   d (159)
8.   a (160)
9.   c (161)
10. d (165)
11. a (166)
12. b (168)
13. c (168)
14. d (168)
15. d (169)

16. d (169)
17. b (172)
18. d (173)
19. c (174)
20. d (174)
21. c (158)
22. b (158)
23. d (160)
24. c (161)
25. c (174)
26. c (169)
27. b (16)
28. c (177)
29. b (177)
30. d (176)

True-False (page references in parentheses)

1.   T (155)
2.   F (156)
3.   F (157)
4.   T (159)
5.   T (161)
6.   F (168)
7.   F (168)
8.   F (179)
9.   T (166)
10. T (175)

CHAPTER 8

NONMARITAL LIVING ARRANGEMENTS: LIVING ALONE, COHABITATION, SAME-SEX COUPLES, AND OTHER OPTIONS

CHAPTER SUMMARY

The distinction between marriage and singlehood has become blurred over the past several decades. As a result, sociologist Catherine Ross has suggested that we need to reconceptualize marital status as a **continuum of social attachment**. Factors such as age, sex, residence, religion, and economic status contribute to the diversity and complexity of single life. The number of singles, or unmarrieds, in the United States has risen strikingly over the past fifty years. The increase in young singles over the past four decades reverses a downward trend lasting from 1900 to 1960. There are three demographic categories of singles, or unmarrieds: the never-married, the divorced, and the widowed. The **sex ratio** is the ratio of men and women in a given society or subgroup of a society. Sex ratios can affect the odds of finding a spouse. Marriage has experienced declining perceived advantages in American society. Much of the increase in singlehood represents a return to long-term patterns of late marriage at the turn of the century; results from economic disadvantage and/or a low sex ratio, which prevent a portion of the population from marrying; and results from changing attitudes toward marriage and singlehood. African Americans have shared in the recent trend toward greater singlehood and scholars have been puzzled by the fact that black marriage rates are substantially lower than those of other groups. The unequal sex ratio among African Americans, as well as black men's high rates of unemployment, underemployment, military service, imprisonment, and other structural factors, works against black people's marrying and contributes to their higher rates of singlehood.

There is evidence that occupation and income are related to marital status. Sociologist Peter Stein sees singles as being discriminated against in subtle ways in the workplace. Satisfaction with single living depends to some extent on income, for financial hardships can impose heavy restrictions.

As unmarrieds make choices about their living arrangements, we see the variety of singles' lives. The number of one-person households has increased dramatically over the past thirty years. Singles have tended to report feeling lonely more often than have marrieds. A growing proportion of young adults are living with one or both parents. The postponement of marriage has meant a longer period of singlehood. Groups of single adults and perhaps children may live together. **Communes** – that is, situations or places characterized by group living – have existed in American society throughout its history. Many gay and lesbian couples live together and share sexual and emotional commitment. In many (other than legal) respects, same-sex relationships are similar to heterosexual ones. **Cohabitation** or singles' living together, gained widespread acceptance over the past forty years so that today heterosexual cohabitants express little concern with cohabitation being a moral issue or with the disapproval of parents or friends. Unmarried couples are generally less homogamous than marrieds. By the mid-1990s, the proportion of nonmarital births to cohabiting heterosexual couples reached about 40 percent. The definition of **domestic partner** usually includes criteria of joint residence and finances, as well as a statement of loyalty and commitment.

Looking at life satisfaction among American adults, surveys since the 1970s have consistently found that, in general, singles of both sexes have been less likely than marrieds to say that they were happy with their lives. Whether a person is single by choice affects satisfaction with singlehood. Although individuals may be single for many reasons, they cannot remain happy for long without support from people they are close to and who care about them. However one chooses to live the single life, maintaining supportive social networks is important.

Chapter 8

LEARNING OBJECTIVES

Based on your careful and thorough reading of Chapter 8, you should:

1. be familiar with the different categories of single people (the never-married, the divorced, and the widowed).

2. be aware of the increasing numbers of singles.

3. understand how attitudes toward marriage and singlehood are changing.

4. be familiar with the "profile" of African-American singles, as well as the meaning of cohabitation among diverse race/ethnic groups.

5. be familiar with the different domestic arrangements of singles (living alone, living with parents, group or communal living, gay and lesbian partners, and domestic partners).

6. understand the distinction between aloneness, loneliness, and how living circumstances affect life satisfaction.

7. appreciate the importance for single people to maintain supportive social networks.

KEY TERMS

civil union (201)
cohabitation (189)
commune (188)
consensual marriage (191)
culture war (200)

Defense of Marriage Act (DOMA) (197)
domestic partner (192)
sex ratio (184)
single (184)

COMPLETION (using key terms)

1. Divorced, widowed, and never-married are subcategories of the term _____.

2. Some cities and corporations have recognized the status of _____ partners who have co-residence, economic cooperation, commitment, and a sense of personal loyalty.

3. Sociologist Catherine Ross has suggested that we need to reconceptualize marital status as a _____ of social attachment.

4. Singles engaging in _____ or living together, has gained widespread acceptance over the past few decades.

5. _____ are situations or places characterized by group living.

6. _____ marriages are heterosexual, conjugal unions that have not gone through a legal marriage ceremony.

7. The _____ is the number of men per 100 women in a group, organization, society, or other collectivity.

8. The status of _____ marriage is a legal doctrine under which persons who live together for a certain period of time, and/or hold themselves out to the community as husband and wife, are in fact "married" – as married as if they had done so "the regular way."

KEY THEORETICAL PERSPECTIVES

the cultural variant vs. the cultural deviant approach to ethnic minority families

INTERNET AND INFOTRAC EXERCISES

Internet Exercises

1. The following link provides an example of model laws and policies that can be used to adopt a **domestic partnerships** plan, http://www.aclu.org/lgbt/relationships/12347res19971231.html
   - What is a "domestic partnership" according to the legal definition?
   - Who are "domestic partners," according to the legal definition?

2. *The Farm* is among the best known communes in the United States. Many other intentional communities have come and gone, but The Farm has endured. Try exploring The Farm's website: http://www.thefarm.org/. Click on "Frequently Asked Questions About the Farm." Then, try clicking on "Our Beliefs." If you have time, you may wish to explore other elements of the web site. After you have completed your "tour," respond to the following questions:
   - In your personal estimation, what are the pros and cons of communal living?
   - Do you think that you would enjoy living in a commune? Why or why not?

3. *Gay Parent Magazine* is a resource for gay men and lesbians who are, and who wish to be, parents. Visit their website: http://www.gayparentmag.com/. Try clicking on some of the components of the current edition of the magazine. Quite likely, there will be articles that address how families are changing. After you have explored this site, respond to the following questions:
   - Gays and lesbians cannot legally marry in the United States, but, as pointed out in this chapter, the laws are changing with regard to gay/lesbian relationships. Gay and lesbian parenting is an even more controversial subject. Endeavoring to maintain your objectivity, and regardless of how you feel about homosexuality, do you think that gays and lesbians can be effective parents? Why or why not?
   - If put to a vote, would you support gay/lesbian marriage? Why or why not?

4. The Alternatives to Marriage Project (AtMP) advocates for equality and fairness for unmarried people, including people who are single, choose not to marry, cannot marry, or live together before marriage. Go to http://www.unmarried.org to learn more about the alternatives project.
   - What are the rights that are promoted at this site?
   - How many people are living with an unmarried partner in the United States?
   - What kinds of discrimination exist for those who cannot or choose not to marry?

Chapter 8

1.   Use the keyword *cohabitation*. Examine a few of the articles that are listed. After you have done this, respond to the following questions:
   • In the not-too-distant past, cohabitation was regarded as a most significant departure from the mainstream value system in American society. Is there any difference between your views on cohabitation and those of your parents? If so, what are the major differences?
   • How do you think cohabitation will be viewed by the next generation (your children, for instance)?

2.   Use the keyword *unmarried couples*. Examine a few of the articles that appear most interesting to you. You might want to focus on laws and legislation dealing with *domestic partnerships*. Summarize in a brief report what you have learned.

3.   Use the keyword *same-sex marriage*. Examine a few of the articles that are cataloged in this category. You may wish to focus on rulings that various churches and/or church bodies have made with regard to this subject. Doing your best to maintain a sense of objectivity, respond to these questions:
   • Do you approve of same-sex marriage? Why or why not?
   • Are you surprised by any of the recent rulings by church-related organizations with respect to same-sex relationships and marriage?

4.   Use the keyword *communal living*. Take a look at as many articles cataloged as you have time for. There should be an article or two relating to the *success* of communes: This would be one way to focus your assessment. Other possibilities are *co-housing* and *middle-class communes*. Write a brief report on what you have learned from this exploration.

MULTIPLE CHOICE

1. _____   The text cites four social factors that may encourage young people today to postpone marriage or not to marry at all. Which of the following is NOT one of these?
   a.   changes in the economy
   b.   improved contraception
   c.   the threat of rising divorce rates
   d.   changing attitudes toward marriage and singlehood

2. _____   One person households have increased as a relative proportion of the population and now make up what portion of the population?
   a.   one-fifth
   b.   half
   c.   one-third
   d.   one-fourth

3. _____   In 2004, what percent of the population aged twenty through twenty-four were living alone?
   a.   74 percent
   b.   54 percent
   c.   7 percent
   d.   20 percent

Mr

4. _____ The number of one-person households now makes up what portion of the population of the United States?
   a.	one-quarter
   b.	one-half
   c.	one-fifth
   d.	one-sixth

5. _____ In the year 2004, there were about 97 men for every 100 women. This statement is an expression of the
   a.	incidence of gender in the population.
   b.	sex quotient.
   c.	sex ratio.
   d.	gender ratio.

6. _____ Which of the following is seen as the first transition into adulthood?
   a.	turning 21
   b.	graduating from high school
   c.	becoming self-supporting
   d.	getting the first job after college

7. _____ During the 1950s, social scientists and people in general tended to characterize singles as
   a.	individualists.
   b.	nonconformists.
   c.	neurotic or unattractive.
   d.	the "beautiful."

8. _____ Research done by the National Marriage Project at Rutgers University found which of the following to be the current trend in the United States?
   a.	marrying after graduation from college
   b.	living alone together
   c.	living with parents until marriage
   d.	deferring marriage until being financially independent

9. _____ Sociologist Frances Goldscheider has pointed out that middle-aged, divorced women with careers tend to look on marriage
   a.	as more desirable than in the past.
   b.	as a "renewable contract."
   c.	skeptically, viewing it as a bad bargain once they have gained financial and sexual independence.
   d.	as a possible option.

10. _____ Communal living was most desirable and highly visible during what decade?
   a.	1930s
   b.	1940s
   c.	1950s
   d.	1960s

Chapter 8

11. _____ According to Kathleen Kiernan, at which stage does cohabitation become a socially acceptable living arrangement?
a. just living together
b. living together, cohabitation, and marriage are indistinguishable
c. living together as a form of courtship
d. living together as an alternative to marriage

12. _____ Committed cohabitors can best described as
a. the couples living together as an alternative to marriage.
b. living together as a form of courtship.
c. those living together as a matter of convenience.
d. those living together while in college.

13. _____ By 2000, _____ of young adults aged eighteen through twenty-four lived with their parents.
a. one-quarter
b. one-third
c. more than half
d. over two-thirds

14. _____ From a variety of national surveys, demographers estimate that _____ percent of lesbians are "currently partnered".
a. 4
b. 14
c. 24
d. 44

15. _____ Today, approximately _____ million U.S. heterosexual couples cohabit.
a. 1.5
b. 3.5
c. 4.5
d. 5.5

16. _____ Because few states allow for inheritance without a will, which of the following is legal?
a. surviving partners receive everything
b. all property becomes that of the state
c. a legal right to ownership of property must be established
d. the deceased partner's family get everything

17. _____ The unmarried parents (who are cohabiting) of one of the partner's children should consider executing three documents. Which of the following is NOT one of these?
a. a Co-parenting Agreement
b. a Living Trust
c. a Nomination of Guardianship
d. a Consent to Medical Treatment

18. _____ By the mid-1990s, the proportion of nonmarital births to cohabiting heterosexual couples reached about _____ percent.
   a. 10
   b. 20
   c. 30
   d. 40

19. _____ Looking at life satisfaction among American adults, surveys since the 1970s have consistently found that, in general, singles of both sexes have been _____ likely than marrieds to say that they were happy with their lives.
   a. far more
   b. somewhat more
   c. less
   d. equally

20. _____ The text points out that when we think of singlehood as a(n) _____, we realize that not all singles are socially unattached, disconnected, or isolated.
   a. finite distribution
   b. continuum
   c. infinite distribution
   d. subculture

21. _____ Which of the following is not a demographic category of the growing number of singles?
   a. never married
   b. divorced
   c. undesirable
   d. widowed

22. _____ According to the text which of the following is NOT a cultural change that has occurred in the last few decades?
   a. attitudes toward nonmarital sex
   b. greater weight given to personal autonomy
   c. emphasis on career rather than family
   d. unmarried is an acceptable alternative to marriage

23. _____ Living situations in shared housing complexes, and sharing meals and recreational activities is typical of _____.
   a. suburban neighborhoods
   b. inner city apartment complexes
   c. communes
   d. college dormitories

24. _____ Of the four stages of cohabitation, Stephanie Coontz identified the United States as being in which stage?
   a. between stage one and two
   b. transitioning between stage two to stage three
   c. stage four
   d. stage three

25. _____ Historically, Puerto Rican women have what kind of relationships?
   a.   cohabitation without a plan to marry
   b.   consensual marriages
   c.   married in formal ceremonies
   d.   nonmarried

26. _____ Cohabiting relationships may deal with all of the following EXCEPT
   a.   lack of commitment
   b.   struggle to define their relationship
   c.   lack of social support
   d.` clearly defined norms to guide behavior

27. _____ Which country was the first to allow same sex couples to marry?
   a.   Canada
   b.   Sweden
   c.   Netherlands
   d.   Norway

28. _____ The alternative to legal marriage for gays and lesbians is
   a.   cohabitation union.
   b.   domestic partnership.
   c.   civil union.
   d.   legalized partnerships.

29. _____ In Catherine Ross's research, a most important finding was that
   a.   people in relationships, married or not, were happier than those not in relationships.
   b.   the happiest in the continuum of relationships were those in long term marriages.
   c.   being single was highly correlated with deep depression.
   d.   unattached singles reported strongest networks of friends.

30. _____ All of the following are sources of support for singles EXCEPT
   a.   families of origin
   b.   volunteer work groups
   c.   group-living situations
   d.   competitive activities

TRUE-FALSE

1. _____ To social scientists, "single" still means "unmarried."

2. _____ In fact, sex ratios have little or no effect on the odds of finding a spouse.

3. _____ Historically, the United States had more women than men.

4. _____ A majority of young adults experience less parental pressure to marry than in the past.

5. _____ The text points out that more women are voluntarily choosing singlehood.

6. _____ The proportion of married African Americans has increased sharply.

7. _____ Singlehood may be freely chosen, imposed by a structural lack of options, self-imposed, or a result of some combination of these.

8. _____ Puerto Rican women have a long history of consensual marriages.

9. _____ The number of one-person households has declined dramatically over the past twenty-five years.

10. _____ Singles are less likely to return home when their parents have been divorced or remarried.

11. _____ Gays and lesbians are likely to adopt traditional masculine and feminine roles in their relationships.

12. _____ The lack of social support for cohabitation may negatively impact the stability of the relationship.

13. _____ The prevalence of cohabitation rises with education.

14. _____ Seventy to 90 percent of people registering domestic partnerships have been heterosexual couples.

15. _____ Whether a person is single by choice affects satisfaction with singlehood.

SHORT ANSWER

1. What are the three demographic categories of singles?

2. What factors contribute to the diversity and complexity of single life?

3.   What are *consensual marriages*? Give several examples.

4.   What are *communes*? Give several examples.

5.   Define *domestic partner*. Give several examples.

ESSAY

1. Define the sex ratio. What is the sex ratio in American society today? How does the sex ratio affect the institution of marriage?

2. Based on the text's discussion, summarize the changing attitudes toward marriage and singlehood.

3. What are the apparent advantages and disadvantages of cohabitation?

4. What is a *domestic partnership*? Give at least one example to support your answer. How are gay and lesbian partners affected by domestic partnerships?

5. What problems do older single adults face that are not faced by younger singles? How are these problems different for men and for women?

Chapter 8

ANSWERS TO SAMPLE QUESTIONS

Completion (using key terms)

1. single
2. domestic
3. continuum
4. cohabitation
5. Communes

6. Consensual
7. sex ratio
8. common law

Multiple Choice (page references in parentheses)

1. c (184-185,188)
2. d (186)
3. c (187)
4. a (186)
5. c (238-239)
6. c (186)
7. c (186)
8. b (187)
9. c (185)
10. d (188-189)
11. b (190)
12. a (191)
13. c (187)
14. d (196)
15. d (189)

16. c (192)
17. b (193)
18. d (195)
19. c (202)
20. b (196)
21. c (184)
22. c (185)
23. d (188-189)
24. b (190)
25. b (191)
26. d (194)
27. c (200)
28. c (201)
29 a (203)
30. d (203-204)

True-False (page references in parentheses)

1. T (184)
2. F (184)
3. F (184)
4. T (186)
5. T (186)
6. F (186)
7. T (184)
8. T (191)

9. F (204)
10. T (188)
11. F (196)
12. T (194)
13. F (194)
14. T (192)
15. T (203)

CHAPTER 9

CHOOSING A MARRIAGE PARTNER, AND THE FIRST YEARS OF MARRIAGE

CHAPTER SUMMARY

By getting married, the majority of American partners accept the responsibility to keep each other primary in their lives. Essentially, this is the **marriage premise**, which consists of permanence and primariness. **Covenant marriage** is a fairly new type of legal marriage in which the bride and groom agree to be bound by a marriage contract that will not let them get divorced as easily as is presently allowed. States have long been invested in marriage and, more recently, have promoted marriage education. State marriage initiatives began after 1996 when the Temporary Assistance for Needy Families (TANF), or "welfare reform" program, was begun. Three subcultural exceptions to norms of sexual exclusivity are swinging, polyamory, and polygamy. Marriage involves the expectations of **primariness**, which includes expectations of **sexual exclusivity**.

Anthropologists have defined kinship as the social organization of the entire family, including blood (**consanguineous**) relatives and **conjugal** relationships acquired through marriage. For most Americans, the **dominant dyad** is marriage. Parsons writes that kinship in the United States is comprised of "interlocking conjugal families" in which married people are common members of their **family of orientation** and of their **family of procreation**. There are social class differences in terms of kinship obligations and marriage relationships (**parallel vs. interactional relationship patterns**).

Social scientist William Doherty has documented the historical change from marriage as a *social institution* to marriage as *"psychological."* Institutional families can be characterized by *responsibility*, their principal value. The chief value of the psychological marriage is satisfaction. The pluralistic family has no one structure or form. Families may now take many forms.

Many gay male and lesbian couples live together in long-term, committed relationships. Gay and lesbian couples may establish families with children by becoming parents through adoption, foster care, planned sexual intercourse, or artificial insemination. In the United States, the 1974 U.S. Supreme Court decision in *Singer v. Hara* defined marriage as a union between one man and one woman. Hawaii and Vermont have enacted, respectively, the **Reciprocal Beneficiaries Law** and the **Civil Union Act**. Pro-gay/lesbian-rights critics argue that these marriage-not-quite rulings are unconstitutional. The Defense of Marriage Act is a federal statute declaring marriage to be a "legal union of one man and one woman." Having first emerged as a remote possibility in the 1970s, legal marriage for gay and lesbian couples became a front-line issue after 1991 when gay activists formed the Equal Rights Marriage Fund.

Given today's high divorce rate, there has been increasing concern that individuals be better prepared for a marital relationship. Today, we view early marriage as a time of role making rather than role taking. A marriage relationship fulfils both practical and intimacy needs. Taboos against **extramarital sex** are widespread among the world's cultures. Although a large majority of Americans publicly disapprove of extramarital sex, in practice, the picture is somewhat different. Computer technology has created **cyberadultery**. The biosocial perspective and exchange theory have been applied in explaining the reasons for extramarital affairs. There are numerous negative effects of extramarital affairs and recovery may be difficult.

One option is to actively pursue an adaptable marriage relationship: one that allows and encourages partners to grow and change. Couples should ask a number of basic questions as they approach these agreements, including such areas as how money and household chores will be allocated, marital goals, and attitudes.

LEARNING OBJECTIVES

Based on your careful and thorough reading of Chapter 9, you should:

1.   be able to define process of mate selection and be familiar with the expectations of stability, divorce risk, and the risks of mate selection.

2.   be familiar with arranged and free-choice marriage and the marital exchange.

3.   be familiar with the dimensions of homogamy, heterogamy and marital stability.

4.   understand the premarital relationship and the transition to marriage, the role of physical attractiveness and rapport

5.   be familiar with the controversy and issues associated with cohabitation and marital quality and stability

6.   understand the key correlates of marital satisfaction and the choices that couples make throughout life.

7.   understand the preparation needed for marriage, adaptable to marriage in the early years, creating a couple connection and creating adaptable relationships.

KEY TERMS (page references in parentheses)

adaptable marriage relationship (229)
arranged marriage (211)
assortative mating (214)
bride price (213)
courtship (220)
cross-national marriage (212)
date rape (acquaintance rape) (221)
dowry (213
endogamy (214)
experience hypothesis (225)
free-choice culture (212)
geographic availability (215)
heterogamy (214)
homogamy (214)

hypergamy (217)
hypogamy (217)
interethnic marriage (217)
interracial marriage (217)
marital stability (206)
marriage market (211)
mate selection risk (211)
pool of eligibles (214)
rape myth (221)
role-making (227)
selection hypothesis (226)
status exchange hypothesis (218)
theory of complementary needs (222)

COMPLETION (using key terms)

1. _____ marriages are those where the parents have chosen the children's future spouses.

2. The United States is a _____culture where people choose their own mates..

3. The money or property that is paid to the family of the bride is a _____.

4. Marrying someone within one's own social group is known as _____.

5. _____ refers to modifying or adjusting the expectations and obligations traditionally associated with a role.

6. _____ is marrying someone who is dissimilar in race, age, education, religion or social class.

7. _____ refers to marriages in which a spouse improves his/her social status by marrying up.

8. The theory of _____ needs is when we are attracted to partners whose needs complement our own.

9. _____ refers to modifying or adjusting the expectations and obligations traditionally associated with a role.

10. A(n) _____ marriage relationship allows and encourages partners to grow and change.

KEY THEORETICAL PERSPECTIVES

Exchange theory
Theory of complementary needs
the biosocial perspective on extramarital affairs
the exchange approach to extramarital affairs

INTERNET AND INFOTRAC EXERCISES

Internet Exercises

1. Many articles, books, seminars, videos, and workshops have been variously entitled "How to Build a Successful Marriage." Formulas for marital happiness have been proposed by a variety of so-called marriage "experts." The *Association for Couples in Marriage Enrichment (ACME)* was founded by David and Vera Mace, who are recognized as serious scholars within the field of marriage and family living. ACME maintains a website at http://www.bettermarriages.org/. Go to the site and examine its contents. Try taking the "Love-Then and Now" exercise: http://www.bettermarriages.org/regexercise.html
   - Do you think that "workshops" and "practical exercises" can help people to build more successful marriages? Why or why not?
   - A commonly heard observation is "Maintaining a happy marriage is hard *work*." Do you think people should have to *work* at having a successful marriage? Why or why not?
   - Whether you are married or not, would you consider attending a "marriage workshop?" State your reasons one way or the other.

2.   The issues surrounding *same-sex marriage* continue to generate a great deal of controversy. There are a number of organizations nationwide, and internationally, that are devoted to lobbying in the interest of equal rights for gay men and lesbians and, more specifically, toward legalizing homosexual marriage. One such organization is the Legal Marriage Alliance of Washington. The LMA maintains a website at http://www.lmaw.org/. Go to the site and browse the contents. After you have familiarized yourself with the issues, respond to the following questions:

- How do *you* feel about same-sex marriage? Have your readings in the textbook and your experiences in this exercise changed your point of view in any way? If so, how?
- Do you think that same-sex marriage will ever be legalized in American society? Why or why not?
- Suppose that medical science eventually provides convincing empirical evidence that sexual orientation is a *biological phenomenon* and that homosexuals and bisexuals have no *choice* in the matter. Do you think this will alter people's perceptions of homosexuality and/or bisexuality? Why or why not?

3.   The following website provides a variety of links that relate to *covenant marriage*: http://www.divorcereform.org/cov.html#anchor1282489 Quite obviously, there are far more sites listed than you will have time to investigate. Focus on those links that discuss the more general aspects of this subject, including the history of the concept. After you have browsed these sites, respond to the following questions:

- What are your personal feelings regarding covenant marriage. Would you consider entering into such an agreement? Why or why not?
- Regardless of your personal point of view about covenant marriage, do you feel that this type of agreement is effective in avoiding divorce? Why or why not?

4.   There are many issues regarding marrying someone from a different religion or faith group. At the following site, http://www.religioustolerance.org/ifm_menu.htm, religious tolerance of different faiths and beliefs is promoted. There are several major issues that are addressed at this site. After reading the issues, answer the following questions.

- Are divorce rates different among mixed marriages?
- How can couples best handle their religious differences?
- What are the policies of different religious and faith groups?

InfoTrac Exercises

1.   Use the keyword *extramarital sex*. Choose several articles to examine more closely. After you have done this, respond to the following:

- Describe the prevailing attitudes toward extramarital sex in American society.
- What are your *personal* feelings about extramarital sex? How does your point of view compare to the points of view in the articles you examined?

2.   Use the keyword *gay parents*. Focus on articles that deal with the legality of gays and lesbians adopting children. After you have examined these sources, respond to the following questions:

- On what grounds have gays and lesbians been denied the legal right to adopt children?

- What are your *personal* views on gay parenting? Do you think that children who are reared by gay parents will become homosexual? Do you feel that the law should prohibit adoption by gays and lesbians? Why or why not?

3.   Use the keyword *prenuptial agreements*. Select several articles based on your personal interests with this subject. After you have read these articles, respond to the following questions:

- The typical reaction to the concept of the prenuptial agreement is that such an arrangement seems to "invite divorce". Do you agree with this point of view? Why or why not?
- Most business partners will testify to the functions of a legal agreement, including the point that should they decide to dissolve their partnership, the agreement will allow them to "go on being friends". Why do you think it is so difficult for people to apply this logic to marriage?

MULTIPLE CHOICE

1. _____   Three of the following are factors in mate selection and marital stability. Which of the following is NOT one of these?
   a.   personality traits
   b.   social connections
   c.   partner interactions
   d.   stability

2. _____   According to attachment theory, individuals who have their needs met as children will
   a.   trust that their relationships will provide ongoing emotional support.
   b.   will worry that their beloved will leave them.
   c.   are dependent upon their partners for security.
   d.   not be trustworthy as partners.

3. _____   Children of divorce are more likely to get divorced because of all of the following EXCEPT
   a.   serious personality problems.
   b.   lack of supportive communication skills.
   c.   commitment to the marriage.
   d.   accepting attitudes toward divorce.

4. _____   Youths who are from divorced families are more likely to select high risk partners. This is known as
   a.   faulty mate selection.
   b.   free choice.
   c.   mutual trait selection.
   d.   mate selection risk.

5. _____   The United States has what is known as a(n) _____ culture.
   a.   open marriage culture
   b.   free-choice
   c.   arranged marriage
   d.   free market

6. _____   The type of open marriage that allows individuals from different countries to wed is
   a.   international marriage trade.
   b.   inter ethnic marriage.
   c.   intra ethnic marriage.
   d.   cross national marriage.

7. _____   In many cultures, the groom must pay a sum of money or property to the bride's family. This is known as a
   - a.   bride price.
   - b.   dowry.
   - c.   kinship bond.
   - d.   marriage exchange.

8. _____   In the Maasai tribes of Kenya, the groom must pay the bride's family five cows for the privilege of marrying their daughter. This is an example of a
   - a.   dowry.
   - b.   family bond.
   - c.   bride price.
   - d.   marriage fee.

9. _____   A Chinese woman and American man marry. This is an example of
   - a.   international marriage trade.
   - b.   inter ethnic marriage.
   - c.   intra ethnic marriage.
   - d.   cross national marriage.

10. _____   The practice of marrying within one's own social group is
   - a.   heterogamy.
   - b.   cenogamy.
   - c.   endogamy.
   - d.   exogamy.

11. _____   Heterogamy involves marrying someone who is all of the following EXCEPT
   - a.   of a different race.
   - b.   of the same religion.
   - c.   is twenty years older.
   - d.   lives in a different country.

12. _____   Which theory is most appropriate for explaining the rewards and costs of a relationship?
   - a.   functionalist
   - b.   attachment
   - c.   allocation
   - d.   exchange

13. _____   The phenomenon of sharing certain social characteristics with one's spouse is
   - a.   heterogamy.
   - b.   homogamy.
   - c.   exogamy.
   - d.   endogamy.

14. _____   There are certain elements that are part of homogamy. Which of the following is NOT one of these?
   - a.   peer pressure
   - b.   geographic availability.
   - c.   social pressure
   - d.   feeling at home

15. _____ When an individual has "married up" or improved their social status, this is known as
    a.   exogamy.
    b.   hypergamy.
    c.   homogamy.
    d.   heterogamy.

16. _____ When it is said that someone has married beneath themselves or married someone from a lower social class, this is an example of
    a.   hypogamy.
    b.   hypergamy.
    c.   homogamy.
    d.   heterogamy.

17. _____ Occasionally individuals will trade their socially defined superior status and marry someone from a less privileged racial or ethnic group. This is the
    a.   exchange theory.
    b.   alternative status theory.
    c.   status exchange hypothesis.
    d.   social transition hypothesis.

18. _____ Marital stability can be measured in terms of two related but different factors. One is stability and the other is
    a.   the length of the marriage.
    b.   marriage maintenance.
    c.   marriage contractual length.
    d.   the happiness of the partners.

19. _____ In a relationship, when a coercive sexual encounter occurs this is known as
    a.   a sexual threat.
    b.   sexual abuse.
    c.   acquaintance rape.
    d.   sexual deviance.

20. _____ When we are attracted to those whose strengths are harmonious with our own, this is an example of
    a.   the theory of complementary needs.
    b.   homogamous mate selection theory.
    c.   the theory of alternative status.
    d.   the status blending theory.

21 _____ According to research, which of the following is a predictor of violence in a dating relationship?
    a.   a history of long term marriages in their family of origin
    b.   a history of domestic violence in their family of origin
    c.   a person is generous with praise
    d.   a person rewards are greater than the costs of the relationship

22. _____ Research regarding cohabitation has shown that
    a.   marriages preceded by more than one instance of cohabitation are more likely to end in separation or divorce.
    b.   cohabitation is positively correlated with long term marriage.
    c.   there is little relationship between cohabitation and a successful marriage.
    d.   younger adults who cohabit are less tolerant of divorce.

23. _____ The process of serial cohabitation that assumes individuals who choose serial cohabitation are different from those who do not is known as
   a.   premarital cohabitation theory.
   b.   experience hypothesis.
   c.   selection hypothesis.
   d.   relationship success hypothesis.

24. _____ Premarital counseling serves all of the following purposes EXCEPT
   a.   helping the couple develop a realistic vision for their marriage.
   b.   making the potential partners aware of possible problems.
   c.   teach ways of communicating.
   d.   convincing them of the importance of counseling.

25. _____ All of the following are potentially problematic topics for couples in their first year of marriage EXCEPT
   a.   balancing job and family.
   b.   sexual frequency.
   c.   deciding on how many children to have.
   d.   agreeing on how much time to spend with each other.

26. _____ A marital relationship that allows and encourages partners to grow and change is
   a.   an adaptable marriage relationship.
   b.   one that has a prenuptial agreement.
   c.   a marriage that follows an long courtship.
   d.   a marriage with common outside interests.

27. _____ If a partner decides to end the relationship, they should do all of the following EXCEPT
   a.   plan the break up.
   b.   decide that breaking up is the right thing to do.
   c.   offer no explanations for the decision.
   d.   prepare themselves for wavering.

28. _____ Physical violence in relationships occurs in
   a.   30 to 50% of relationships.
   b.   20 to 40% of relationships.
   c.   25 to 35% of relationships.
   d.   40 to 50% of relationships.

29. _____ The beliefs about rape that function to blame the victim and exonerate the rapist are
   a.   rape truths.
   b.   facts about sexual coercion.
   c.   rape myths.
   d.   rape lies.

30. _____ The old-fashioned term used to describe the process through which couples develop mutual commitment and progresses toward marriage is
   a.   spooning.
   b.   dating.
   c.   keeping company.
   d.   courtship.

TRUE-FALSE

1. _____ Expectations for stability are associated with marital satisfaction.

2. _____ The intergenerational transmission of divorce influences the success of marriages of children.

3. _____ Exogamy is a marriage arrangement demanding sexual fidelity.

4. _____ Arranged marriages allow for multiple wives for one husband.

5. _____ Cohabitating couples generally expect each other to be sexually faithful.

6. _____ Homogamy offers the widest selection of possible mates.

7. _____ Geographic availability is the same as propinquity.

8. _____ Marital success is measured by stability and the happiness of the partners.

9. _____ Interethnic and interracial marriages are the same.

10. _____ Complementary needs are those that are the same for each partner.

11. _____ Dating violence occurs in over half of the dating relationships.

12. _____ Role-making refers to modifying or adjusting expectations associated with a role.

SHORT ANSWER

1. What are the factors associated with marital stability?.

2. Distinguish between an arranged marriage and a free choice marriage. Give an example of each.

3.   What is the difference between exogamy and endogamy? Give an example of each.

4.   What is homogamy and what are the reasons for homogamy?

5.   What is date rape, or acquaintance rape, and what are the warning signs?

ESSAY

1. What is the *marriage premise*? How does this concept relate to expectations of permanence and expectations of primariness? Give a practical example of the marriage premise.

2. Describe the transition from marriage as institution to pluralistic families. Give several examples to support your answer.

3. Compare and contrast the views of gay rights activists and the American public on the issue of same-sex marriage. How does the Defense of Marriage Act fit in here?

4. Based on the text's discussion, what are the primary correlates of marital satisfaction? How are "couple connections" created?

5. What are the primary components of an *adaptable marriage relationship*? List at least four questions that couples should pose if they want to achieve this kind of relationship.

Chapter 9

ANSWERS TO SAMPLE QUESTIONS

Completion (using key terms)

1. Arranged
2. free choice
3. bride price
4. homogamy
5. Role-making

6. Heterogamy
7. Hypergamy
8. complementary needs
9. Role-making
10. adaptable

Multiple Choice (page references in parentheses)

1. b (208)
2. a (209)
3. c (210)
4. d (211)
5. b (212)
6. c (212)
7. a (213)
8. c (213)
9. d (212)
10. c (214)
11. b (214)
12. d (213)
13. a (214)
14. b (215)
15. b (217)
16. a (217)

17. c (218)
18. d (219)
19. c (221)
20. a (222)
21. b (224)
22. d (225)
23. c (226)
24. d (227)
25. c (228)
26. a (229)
27. c (223)
28. b (223)
29. c (221)
30. d (220)

True-False (page references in parentheses)

1. T (208)
2. T (210)
3. F (214)
4. F (211)
5. T (225)
6. F (214)

7. T (215)
8. T (219)
9. F (217)
10. F (222)
11. F (224)
12. T (227)

CHAPTER 10

TO PARENT OR NOT TO PARENT

CHAPTER SUMMARY

This chapter explores the causes and consequences of individual and collective decisions and behavior related to **fertility** rates – factors that play a part in parenting and population size, growth and decline.

Significant changes have taken place in American childbearing patterns over the past decades. As overall fertility levels have dropped, childbearing has increasingly shifted to later ages. Lower fertility appears to be a major change when we compare current birth rates to those of the 1950s. Fertility rates vary among segments of the U.S. population. Differential birth rates reflect the fact that beliefs and values about having children vary among cultures and among the general population. African Americans, Hispanics, Asian Americans, and Native Americans display many differences in fertility and fertility rates.

Today, individuals have more choice than ever about whether, when, and how many children to have. Although parenthood has become more of an option, there is no evidence of an embracing childlessness. Our society still has a **pronatalist bias**. The majority of Americans continue to value parenthood, believe that childbearing should accompany marriage, and feel social pressure to have children. Only a very small percentage view childlessness as an advantage, regard the decision not to have children as a positive, believe that the ideal family is one without children, or expect to be childless by choice. Nevertheless, it is likely that changing values concerning parenthood, the weakening of social norms prescribing marriage and parenthood, a wider range of alternatives for women, the desire to postpone marriage and childbearing, and the availability of modern contraceptives and legal abortion will eventually result in a higher proportion of Americans remaining childless. In fact, some observers have begun to worry that American society may be drifting into a period of **structural antinatalism**.

Children can add a fulfilling and highly rewarding experience to people's lives, but they also impose complications and stresses, both financial and emotional. Couples today are faced with options other than the traditional family of two or more children, remaining childless, postponing parenthood until they are ready, and having only one child. Often, people's decisions concerning having a family are made by default. Although pregnancy outside of marriage has increased, many unmarried pregnant women choose **abortion**. There are many social and ethical issues surrounding the technologies and behaviors related to contraception and abortion.

Involuntary infertility has been influenced, as have other issues, by rapid changes in reproductive technology that have given rise to social and ethical issues. More and more, **assisted reproductive technology (ART)** has become a normal part of reproduction. Choosing to use reproductive technology depends on one's values and circumstances.

Public and private; open and closed **adoption** are ways of becoming a parent without conceiving; some families have both adopted and biological children. The majority of adoptions of older and disabled children work out well. International adoption has grown dramatically in recent years.

Chapter 10

LEARNING OBJECTIVES

Based on your careful and thorough reading of Chapter 10, you should:

1. be familiar with recent fertility trends in the United States.

2. understand the social pressures associated with having children and the dynamics surrounding the decision to parent or not to parent.

3. be acquainted with the three emerging options involving parenthood: remaining child-free, postponing parenthood, and the one-child family.

4. be familiar with the history of and the issues surrounding the prevention of pregnancy.

5. be familiar with the issues involved in pregnancy outside of marriage.

6. be acquainted with the politics, social attitudes about, safety, and the emotional and psychological impact of abortion.

7. understand the issues surrounding involuntary infertility and the solutions offered by reproductive technology.

8. be familiar with the adoption process, including the adoption of racial/ethnic minority children, older children, and international adoption.

KEY TERMS (page references in parentheses)

abortion (252)
assisted reproductive technology
    [ART] (255)
attachment disorder (260)
fecundity (234)
fertility (234)
impaired fertility (255)
induced abortion (252)
informal adoption (258)
involuntary infertility (254)
multipartnered fertility (251)

opportunity costs
    [of children] (242)
pronatalist bias (240)
replacement level [of fertility] (236)
single mothers by choice (249)
social capital perspective
    [on parenthood] (241)
structural antinatalism (240)
total fertility rate [TFR] (234)
value of children perspective
    [on parenthood] (241)
voluntary childlessness (243)

COMPLETION (using key terms)

1. The _____ rate is the number of births a typical woman will have over her lifetime.

2. _____ describes the physical inability to have children.

3. The text points out that our society still has a _____: Having children is taken for granted, whereas not having children must be justified.

4. Added to the direct costs of parenting are _____ costs: the economic opportunities for wage earning and investments that parents forgo when rearing children.

5. The *value of children perspective* has more recently been supplemented by a _____ perspective on the benefits of parenthood.

6. _____ is the condition of wanting to conceive and bear a child, but being physically unable to do it.

7. _____ refers to the procedure where one couple's unneeded frozen embryos are used to enable another couple to have a child.

8. When _____ adoption is employed, children are taken into a parent's house, but the adoption is not legally formalized.

9. _____ involve the meeting of birth parents, most often the mother, with the biological child.

10. In cases of _____, adoptive children defensively shut off the willingness or ability to make future attachments to anyone.

KEY THEORETICAL PERSPECTIVES

the demographics of fertility

INTERNET AND INFOTRAC EXERCISES

<u>Internet Exercises</u>

1. Go to: http://www.bellaonline.com/articles/art683.asp. After you have read the article, click on the link "Some Parents Regret Having Kids." Following your review of these materials, respond to the following questions:
    *   What kinds of questions should couples pose in evaluating whether they want to have children?
    *   Being as objective as you can, does it make you feel uncomfortable that many men and women are having children for "all of the wrong reasons?" Ask *yourself* the questions alluded to in the web site. What is the result?

2. Go to: http://www.policyalmanac.org/health/archive/hhs_teenage_pregnancy.shtml. After you have perused the contents of this website, respond to the following questions:
    *   How does the Department of Health and Human Services target the problem of adolescent pregnancy?
    *   What types of health and human services programs are in place to combat adolescent/teenage pregnancy?

3. The National Abortion and Reproductive Rights Action League (NARAL) is devoted to women's right to choose abortion. Their website may be found at: http://www.naral.org/. The American Life League is the nation's largest grassroots pro-life educational organization. Their website may be found at: http://www.all.org/. Take a look at each website and briefly familiarize yourself with the contents. Then, respond to the following questions:

- What are the primary differences between the *pro-choice* and *pro-life* agendas?
- Use this opportunity as an exercise in sociological objectivity. Regardless of your *personal* ideological stance, which website do you find the most convincing? Why?
- What is your *personal* position in reference to the *pro-choice/pro-life* debate? How do you justify your point of view?

4.   The U.S. Department of State offers advice on international adoptions at http://travel.state.gov/family/adoption/adoption_485.html. With the increasing numbers of individuals who are choosing international adoptions the information is invaluable.
- What can the state department do for couples?
- What are the things the state department cannot do for couples?

InfoTrac Exercises

1.   Use the keyword *childlessness*. Select two or three of the articles listed that you find particularly interesting and read the contents. Then respond to the following questions:
- Do you think that human beings are "inborn parents?" Why or why not? Particularly in the case of women, do you think there is some type of "mothering instinct?" Should a woman who is *not* enthusiastic about having children feel that there is something wrong with her? Why or why not?
- Do you think men and women who become fathers and mothers always *want* to have children? If not, then what are some of the other motivations that people have for becoming parents?
- How do *you* feel about having children? Have you thought *critically* and *analytically* about your reasons for wanting (or not wanting) children? What are those reasons?

2.   Use the keywords *interracial adoption*. Select two or three articles that interest you and then respond to these questions:
- What are your reactions to interracial/transracial adoption? If you object, what are your reasons?
- Do you think that the *children* in interracial/transracial adoption situations suffer any negative consequences? If so, what kind?
- If you were adopting, would you consider a child who belongs to a different race? Why or why not?

3.   Use the key words *multiple birth*. Select two or three articles that you find particularly interesting and read the contents. Then, respond to the following questions:
- If you were experiencing infertility problems, would you consider drug therapy that could produce multiple births? Why or why not?
- Based on the text's discussion of fertility, what are the *demographic* implications of infertility drugs and multiple births? Do you think that there is any cause for concern in terms of world population? Why or why not?

4.   Use the key words *in vitro fertilization: where should you draw the line?* After you have read the contents of the article listed, respond to the following questions:
- Do you think there should be any legal limitations regarding the employment of in vitro fertilization? If so, what should these limitations entail?
- If you experienced infertility problems, would you consider in vitro fertilization as an option? Why or why not?

MULTIPLE CHOICE

1. _____   In recent years, the total fertility rate has fluctuated around
   a.   1.0.
   b.   2.0.
   c.   3.0.
   d.   4.0

2. _____   In general, which family category is likely to have fewer children?
   a.   affluent and highly educated
   b.   middle-class
   c.   working-class
   d.   the poor

3. _____   By the _____, the birthrate among blacks had become very close to that of whites.
   a.   1850s
   b.   1880s
   c.   1930s
   d.   1960s

4. _____   The lifetime fertility rate of Latinas varies strongly with
   a.   age.
   b.   socioeconomic status.
   c.   educational attainment.
   d.   country of origin.

5. _____   Some observers argue that U.S. society has become _____ – that is, against having children or, at least, that it is not doing all it can to support parents and their children.
   a.   child disoriented
   b.   antinatalist
   c.   child-opposed
   d.   child-phobic

6. _____   The average cost of rearing a child born in 2001 to age eighteen is estimated at _____ for middle-income families.
   a. $58,470
   b. $128,470
   c. $178,470
   d. $231,470

7. _____   In husband-wife families with two children, an estimated _____ percent of household expenses are attributable to children.
   a.   22
   b.   32
   c.   42
   d.   72

8. _____   At present, it appears that _____ percent of women choose voluntary childlessness.
   a.   12
   b.   10
   c.   8
   d.   6

9. _____ The text points out that, over time, spouses' reported marital satisfaction tends to
  a. decline over time.
  b. increase somewhat over time.
  c. remain stable.
  d. increases dramatically over time.

10. _____ The text observes that individuals who choose to remain childless
  a. are frustrated.
  b. are unhappy.
  c. typically have vital relationships.
  d. often believe that adding a third member to their family would end their relationship.

11. _____ Sylvia Ann Hewlett's book, *Creating a Life* was based on her survey of over one-thousand
  a. upper-class men.
  b. high-achieving career women.
  c. lower-middle class women.
  d. working-class women.

12. _____ In 2002, _____ percent of women experiencing a first birth were married to the father.
  a. 30
  b. 40
  c. 50
  d. 60

13. _____ In 2002, _____ percent of African American births occurred outside marriage.
  a. 28
  b. 38
  c. 68
  d. 98

14. _____ Marital and nonmarital birth rates are highest among which of the following groups?
  a. African Americans
  b. Asian Americans
  c. Native Americans
  d. Hispanics

15. _____ Which of the following has the highest teen pregnancy, abortion, and birth rates of any industrialized country?
  a. China
  b. Great Britain
  c. the United States
  d. Russia

16. _____ Since 1980, the rate of abortions per 1,000 women of childbearing age (15-44) has
  a. increased dramatically.
  b. increased somewhat.
  c. increased slightly.
  d. decreased.

17. _____ More than half of the abortions performed are
    a.   in the second trimester.
    b.   in a hospital or a clinic.
    c.   in the first nine weeks.
    d.   induced by drugs.

18. _____ Approximately _____ of couples defined as infertile will eventually conceive and deliver, with or without medical intervention.
    a.   one-fourth
    b.   one-third
    c.   one-half
    d.   three-fourths

19. _____ When a couple has not been able to carry a pregnancy to full term, this is called
    a.   infertility.
    b.   impaired fertility.
    c.   secondary infertility.
    d.   primary infertility.

20. _____ At present, _____ of assisted reproductive technology (ART) births are multiples.
    a.   about one-fourth
    b.   one-third
    c.   over one-half
    d.   at least three-fourths

21. _____ The U.S. Census looked at adoption for the first time in
    a.   1950.
    b.   1960.
    c.   1980.
    d.   2000.

22. _____ Louise Brown, the first in vitro fertilization (IVF) baby, turned 25 years old in

    _____.
    a.   2002
    b.   2003
    c.   2004
    d.   2005

23. _____ _____ adoptions take place through licensed agencies.
    a.   Public
    b.   Private
    c.   Open
    d.   Closed

24. _____ In 2000, about _____ adoptions were international (of children outside the country).
    a.   2,000
    b.   6,000
    c.   12,000
    d.   18,000

25. _____ Adoptions arranged between the adoptive parents and the birth mothers are
     a.   private.
     b.   public.
     c.   legal.
     d.   personal.

26. _____ The portion of one child families in America is growing because of
     a.   the high cost of raising a child.
     b.   women's increasing career opportunities.
     c.   negative stereotypes of one-child families.
     d.   peer support to those choosing to have just one child.

27. _____ Which of the following is true about nonmarital births?
     a.   overall childbearing has declined and so have nonmarital births
     b.   nonmarital births are at an all-time high
     c.   nonmarital births increased in the 90s
     d.   nonmarital births accounted for only 5% of babies born in the 80s

28. _____ Multipartnered fertility is a relatively new term that is applied to women who have children with different fathers. This is most common in what type of family?
     a.   second marriages
     b.   third marriages
     c.   nonmarital families
     d.   fragile families

29. _____ In studying fertility history, research has shown that _____ percent of mothers have children by only one father.
     a.   25
     b.   35
     c.   55
     d.   75

30. _____ According to the U.S. Census, _____ have the highest rate of adoption relative to their population.
     a.   Asian/Pacific Islanders
     b.   African Americans
     c.   Hispanics
     d.   white non-Hispanics

TRUE-FALSE

1. _____ In the history of American society, as women's employment increased, fertility declined.

2. _____ Women born during the Depression years of the 1930s favored smaller families.

3. _____ Historically, until the late nineteenth century, American fertility was higher than that of Europe.

4. _____ Usually, more highly educated and well-off families have larger numbers of children.

5. _____ Native American women who live on reservations have significantly lower fertility than those who do not.

6. _____ The text observes that in traditional society, couples didn't decide to have children.

7. _____ The total fertility rate is lower today in all racial/ethnic groups than it was during the baby boom era.

8. _____ There are social pressures to have children but other features of our society make parenthood less than automatic.

9. _____ Marital strain is considered to be a common cost of having children.

10. _____ In the United States, birth rates for women in their thirties and forties are now the lowest seen in three decades.

11. _____ Pregnancies to unmarried women are never planned.

12. _____ There were no actual publications describing birth control techniques until the early 1900s.

13. _____ In 2000, over four-fifths of abortions were obtained by unmarried women.

14. _____ The incidence of involuntary fertility increased substantially during most of the twentieth century.

15. _____ Informal adoption is most common among Alaska Natives, blacks, and Hispanics.

SHORT ANSWER

1. What is the *total fertility rate*? How has this rate changed over the years in the United States? What does this change imply?

2.   How has the status of parenthood been affected by reproductive technology?

3.   Briefly but completely summarize fertility trends in the U.S. since 1800 to the present.

4.   Compare ethnic/minority fertility rates with the non-Hispanic white fertility rate. What similarities/differences can be seen?

5.   What is *assisted reproductive technology* (ART)? Give several examples.

ESSAY

1.   Compare African American, Hispanic, and Asian American fertility rates with the fertility rate of non-Hispanic whites.

2.   Explore parents' costs and benefits of having children, making sure to include in your answer social pressures as one factor that should be considered.

3.   Discuss the issues that characterize transracial and international adoption in U.S. society today.

4.   Write an essay in which you discuss the three emerging options discussed by the text book regarding parenthood: remaining childfree, postponing parenthood, and having one child. For each, be sure to discuss the pros and cons inherent in selecting the option.

5.   Discuss the pros and cons of different types of adoptions (public, private, open, closed, informal, and international).

ANSWERS TO SAMPLE QUESTIONS

Completion (using key terms)

1.   total birth rate
2.   Infecundity or sterility
3.   pronatalist bias
4.   opportunity
5.   social capital

6.   Involuntary infertility
7.   Embryo adoption
8.   informal
9.   Adoption reunions
10. attachment disorder

Multiple Choice (page references in parentheses)

1.   b (234)
2.   a (236)
3.   c (238)
4.   c (239)
5.   b (240)
6.   d (242)
7.   c (274)
8.   d (242)
9.   a (242)
10. c (243)
11. b (245)
12. b (248)
13. c (248)
14. d (249)
15. c (250)

16. a (252)
17. c (252)
18. c (255)
19. d (255)
20. c (255)
21. d (257)
22. b (258)
23. a (259)
24. d (296)
25. a (259)
26. c (246)
27. b (247)
28. c (251)
29. d (251)
30. a (257)

True-False (page references in parentheses)

1.   T (234)
2.   F (236)
3.   T (236)
4.   F (236)
5.   F (239)
6.   T (240)
7.   T (239)
8.   T (240)

9.   T (242)
10. F (249)
11. F (247)
12. F (251)
13. T (252)
14. F (254)
15. T (258)

CHAPTER 11

RAISING CHILDREN IN A MULTICULTURAL SOCIETY

CHAPTER SUMMARY

Although rearing children may be a joyful and fulfilling enterprise, parenting today takes place in a social context that can make child rearing an enormously difficult task. There are both advantages and disadvantages of being a parent today. Middle-aged parents may find they are members of a **sandwich generation**: They have role conflicts between parenting and elder care. **Grandparent families** face special challenges. The **transition to parenthood** is frequently difficult.

There are old and new images of parents. Mothers typically engage in more hands-on parenting and take primary responsibility for children, whereas fathers are often viewed as helping. Couples' commitment to shared parenting varies, depending on a variety of factors, including whether both father and mother are **primary parents**.

Children's needs differ according to their age. Parents and stepparents gradually establish a **parenting style** – a general manner of relating to and disciplining their children. Three main styles have been identified: **authoritarian, laissez-faire,** and **authoritative**. Child psychologists prefer the authoritative style. There is ongoing controversy among pediatricians and social scientists over whether spanking is appropriate, however, the consensus seems to be that spanking should be avoided. There is evidence that a conscientious **para-parent** can generate a resilient child.

Social class standing can affect a parent's options and decisions. The 1996 welfare reforms led to the formation of a new federal program designed to assist needy families: **Temporary Assistance for Needy Families (TANF)**. A majority of poor parents live in rented homes, apartments, or motel rooms and are employed. These "working poor" have minimum- or less-than-minimum wage jobs with irregular and unpredictable hours and no medical insurance or other benefits. Rearing children in poverty is qualitatively different from doing so otherwise. Homeless parents present special problems for childrearing. Blue-collar/working class parents are more likely than middle- and upper-class parents to be strict disciplinarians. Incomes have grown little for middle-class parents. Upper-middle class parents have the money to fit the idealized cultural image of the self-sufficient nuclear family. These parents sometimes place too many demands on their children and produce "hurried" children.

There is racial and ethnic diversity in parenting procedures, but evidence suggests that African Americans, as well as Hispanic and Asian American parents' attitudes, behaviors, and hopes for their children are similar to those of other parents in their social class. Native American parents tend toward a laissez-faire parenting style. Hispanic parents tend toward **hierarchical parenting**. Some Asian Americans adhere to a **Confucian training doctrine**. There are increasing numbers of multiracial children. Parents with minority religions in America hope that their children will remain true to their religious heritage. Parents do not necessarily agree on the best approach to racial issues.

There are three newly visible parenting environments: gay male and lesbian parents, grandparent parents, and foster parents. Gay men and lesbians become parents in various ways. Research suggests that children of gay male and lesbian parents are well adjusted and no different from children of heterosexual parents. More than 3.6 million children under age eighteen are living in a grandparent's household. When state or county officials determine that a child is being abused or neglected, they can take temporary or permanent custody of the children and place him/her in **foster care**. Some foster care takes place in **group homes**. A significant portion of foster care is **family foster care** – foster care that takes place in a trained and licensed foster parent's home. There is also **formal kinship care**, which is out-of-home placement with biological relatives of children who are in the custody of the state. There is a shortage of foster parents today.

Parenting often actively continues with adult children. Parents who anticipated increased intimacy or personal freedom may be disappointed when the nest doesn't empty. Relationships between parents and their children last a lifetime, but range from tight-knit to detached.

Studies show that good parenting involves at least four factors: (1) adequate economic resources; (2) being involved in a child's life and school; (3) using supportive, rather than negative, communication between partners; and (4) having support from family and/or friends.

LEARNING OBJECTIVES

Based on your careful and thorough reading of Chapter 11, you should:

1. be familiar with images of modern parents.

2. be familiar with the transition to parenthood.

3. be acquainted with what mothers and fathers do.

4. understand the concept of shared parenthood.

5. be familiar with the different types of parenting (authoritarian, laissez-faire, and authoritative).

6. be acquainted with the different points of view on spanking and physical discipline.

7. be acquainted with the differences in parenting styles based on social class membership.

8. be familiar with racial/ethnic diversity and parenting.

9. be able to identify the challenges of the newly visible parenting environments.

10. be familiar with the relationships between parents and young-adult children and between independent adults and their parents.

11. know the four factors that are related to better parent-child relationships.

KEY TERMS (page references in parentheses)

authoritarian parenting style (274)
authoritative parenting style (274)
Confucian training doctrine (282)
family foster care (286)
formal kinship care (285)
foster care (446)

grandparent families (285)
group homes (286)
hierarchical parenting (281)
laissez-faire parenting style (274)
para-parent (274)
parenting alliance (272)

parenting style (274)
primary parents (272)
shared parenting (272)

Temporary Assistance for
Needy Families [TANF] (278)
transition to parenthood (268)

COMPLETION (using key terms)

1. A form of parenting that is used when a child from the parental home is _____ care.

2. In _____ families, a grandparent acts as the primary parent for grandchildren.

3. _____ parents refer to a couple "mothering together" rather than one parent and one helper.

4. A _____ style refers to a general manner of relating to and disciplining children.

5. The _____ parenting style is characterized as low on emotional nurturing and support but high on parental direction and control.

6. The _____ parenting style is permissive, allowing children to set their own limits with little or no parental guidance.

7. The _____ parenting style combines emotional nurturing and support with parental direction.

8. The federal program called _____ replaced the Aid to Families with Dependent Children program.

9. _____ parenting combines warm emotional support for children with a demand for significant respect for parents and other authority figures.

10. The _____ doctrine is similar to hierarchical parenting, blending parental love, concern, involvement, and physical closeness with strict and firm control.

11. Some foster care takes place in _____ homes, where several children are cared for round-the-clock by paid professionals who work in shifts and live elsewhere.

12. _____ takes place in a trained and licensed foster parent's home.

13. _____ is out-of-home placement with biological relatives of children who are in the custody of the state.

KEY THEORETICAL PERSPECTIVES

family ecology perspective
interactionist perspective
cultural equivalent approach
cultural variant approach

Chapter 11

INTERNET AND INFOTRAC EXERCISES

<u>Internet Exercises</u>

1.   The text discusses homeless families with children. Go to
      http://www.nationalhomeless.org/publications/facts/families.pdf. This website is sponsored by the
      National Coalition for the Homeless and provides a detailed description of the problems and
      challenges encountered by homeless families with children. After you have read the article,
      respond to the following questions:
      •   What are the primary causes of homeless families with children?
      •   What are the major consequences of homeless families with children?
      •   If you were a policy maker, what suggestions would you propose for dealing with the
              problem of homeless families with children?

2.   The text poses the question, "Is spanking ever appropriate?" In the text's discussion, the research
      of Murray Straus is cited, including Prof. Straus's point that parents should be aware of how
      harmful spanking can be, *even* if the parents are otherwise loving and supportive. There *are* two
      sides of this debate, and a number of investigators do not necessarily agree with Prof. Straus's
      blanket conclusions regarding corporal punishment. To capture a glimpse of this variation, go to
      http://people.biola.edu/faculty/paulp/. There, you will find a series of links to summaries of the
      literature and complete research reports available on PDF files that cover the entire waterfront of
      opinion about this controversial issue. Quite obviously, there is a great deal of information
      available through this particular web link. Select a few of the issues/discussions that you find
      most interesting and investigate them on the Net. Take a look at the work of Larzelere, who has
      actually debated Straus in public forums. Then, respond to the following questions:
      •   Do you support the conclusions of Larzelere or Straus? Why?
      •   Did you receive corporal punishment when you were a child? Consequently, do you think
              your point of view about corporal punishment is related to your *personal* experiences
              with this issue as a child? How?
      •   Some public and private school systems have, with parental consent, *reinstituted* certain
              forms of corporal punishment. Do you think this is positive or negative? Why?

3.   *Foster parenthood* is a topic that has received increased attention in recent years. Go to
      http://www.arvinpublications.com/parenthood.html. There, you will find a number of links that
      will provide you with a glimpse of various aspects of foster parenting. It should not be too time
      consuming to have a look at each link provided. After you have familiarized yourself with the
      issues, respond to the following questions:
      •   Whether you are already a biological parent, or if you plan to have children of your own,
              would you consider becoming a foster parent? Why or why not?
      •   Being as objective as you can, what do you think are the *pros* and *cons* of foster
              parenthood?
      •   Do you think if more people were willing to become foster parents, that some of the
              problems involving American youth today could be dealt with more effectively? Why or
              why not?

4.   The text points to the growing number of senior citizens who are primary parents for their grandchildren. This topic has attracted a great deal of attention recently, including on the Internet. Go to http://www.raisingyourgrandchildren.com/. The opening page offers a variety of subtopics for grandparents as parents. After you have taken a look at these features, respond to the following questions:
  • Are you troubled by the trend toward grandparents acting as parents for their grandchildren? If so, why?
  • What do you think the future will bring with regard to the emerging lifestyle for grandparents who are primarily responsible for the rearing of their grandchildren?
  • Do you think that most grandparents can do a good job of rearing their grandchildren? Why or why not?

5.   Many couples are waiting until their late 30s or even into their 40s to have children. Read the article from the New York Times http://query.nytimes.com/gst/fullpage.html?res=9B0DEFDE1031F935A15752C0A961948260&sec=&spon=&pagewanted=print about those who waited, and the children of parents who were older when they were born.
  • Would you consider deferring childbearing until your late 30s?
  • After reading the article, what do you think are the advantages and disadvantages of becoming parents later in life?
  • Is this fair to the children? What are the pros and cons of this decision for children?

InfoTrac Exercises

1.   Use the key words *marital change during the transition to parenthood*. Read the article written by Donna G. Knauth. After you have read the article, respond to the following questions:
  • What are the key changes identified by the author that married couples are likely to experience with the transition to parenthood?
  • Why does the author believe that pediatric nurses can make a difference in helping new parents adjust to the transition?
  • If you are already a parent, did you experience some of the changes described in the article? If you are not a parent, do you think that you would be affected by any/all of these changes? Why or why not?
  • If you are already a parents, did you experience some of the changes described in the article>? If you are not a parent, do you think that you would be affected by any/all of these changes? Why or why not?

2.   The text discusses parents of biracial children. One of the principal concerns in this regard involves the biracial child's *identity*. The interactionist perspective can be very helpful in analyzing this dimension. Use the key words *biracial children*. You will find a number of interesting articles, some of which deal with the identity of biracial children. Focus on those articles. After you have examined them, respond to the following questions:
  • What kinds of identity problems are biracial children likely to encounter?
  • How can parents help biracial children cope with these identity issues?
  • Do you think that men and women with different racial identities should marry and have children? Why or why not?

3. Use the key words *children of gay parents*. You will find a wide selection of articles that deal with the children of gay parents. Depending upon how much time you have, select one or more of these articles for examination. Then, respond to the following questions:
    - What kinds of challenges are faced by the children of gay parents?
    - Regardless of how you feel about homosexuality, and trying to be as objective as you can, answer the questions "Should gays and lesbians become parents? Why or why not?"
    - Do you think that the children of gay parents suffer negative stigma? If so, do you have any ideas about how this stigma could be avoided?

4. The text discusses Diana Baumrind's typology of parenting styles. The *authoritative* parenting style is generally recognized as the most effective approach. Use the key words *raising competent kids: the authoritative parenting style*. Read Jeanne Ballantine's article. Then, respond to the following questions:
    - What are the advantages of the authoritative parenting style?
    - Based on the text's discussion, how would you characterize the style that *your parents* used in terms of your socialization?
    - If you are planning on having children, what parenting style do you think you will favor?

MULTIPLE CHOICE

1. _____ The text describes three newly visible parenting environments. Which of the following is NOT one of these?
    a. parents and young adult children
    b. grandparents as parents
    c. adoptive parents
    d. foster parents

2. _____ Interviews in two hospitals' labor and delivery units with eighty-eight mothers and seventy-five fathers of firstborns found that _____ expressed worry or concern about becoming parents.
    a. about one-fourth of the fathers and one-third of the mothers
    b. close to one-third of the fathers and one-half of the mothers
    c. nearly all of the fathers and two-thirds of the mothers
    d. nearly all of the fathers and mothers

3. _____ According to Alice Rossi, the transition to parenthood is more difficult than the transition of becoming a worker or a spouse for several reasons. Which of the following is NOT one of these?
    a. Parenting is more challenging than work roles or spousal roles.
    b. Cultural pressure encourages adults to become parents even though they may not really want to.
    c. Most parents approach parenting with little or no previous experience in child care.
    d. Adjusting to parenthood necessitates changes in the couple's relationship.

4. _____ According to the text, recent research has revealed that, throughout history, fatherhood has displayed
    a. flexibility.
    b. rigidity.
    c. alignment with dominant cultural images.
    d. consistent stereotypes.

5. _____ According to the text's discussion of fathers as primary parents,
   a. less than 1 percent of all U.S. children under age fifteen are living with single fathers.
   b. about 1.1 million children under age fifteen live with a single father who is cohabiting.
   c. about 25 percent of black and of Hispanic children live with single fathers.
   d. about 100,000 children under age fifteen are living in two-parent families with a stay-at-home father.

6. _____ As men are beginning to redefine their roles as fathers, they are becoming involved in all of the following day-to-day tasks EXCEPT
   a. doing errands.
   b. sharing activities.
   c. taking children to doctor's appointments.
   d. teaching their children.

7. _____ In her investigations, Diane Ehrensaft found that three factors affected both parents' commitment to shared parenting. Which of the following is NOT one of these?
   a. Many couples were strongly influenced by the feminist movement.
   b. All couples were one-hundred percent committed to egalitarianism.
   c. Many of the fathers were in occupations related to children, such as academic child psychology.
   d. Both parents tended to have good job security.

8. _____ The text distinguishes among three parenting styles. Which of the following is NOT one of these?
   a. punitive
   b. authoritarian
   c. authoritative
   d. laissez-faire

9. _____ Both authoritarian and laissez-faire parenting styles are associated with children's and adolescent's
   a. good mental health.
   b. excellent school performance.
   c. high rates of teen sexuality and pregnancy.
   d. behavioral conformity.

10. _____ _____ parents would agree with the statements "I communicate rules clearly and directly," "I consider my child's wishes and opinions along with my own when making decisions," and "I expect my child to act independently at an age-appropriate level."
   a. Authoritarian
   b. Laissez-faire
   c. Punitive
   d. Authoritative

11. _____ Who, among the following groups of children, are spanked most often?
   a. boys over age five
   b. boys under age two
   c. girls over age five
   d. girls under age two

12. _____ Research by psychologist Marjorie Gunnoe suggests that only _____ are more likely to lie, cheat, or bully others if spanked.
    a. girls between ages five and eight who live with African-American, single mothers
    b. boys between ages seven and ten who live with white, single fathers
    c. boys between ages eight and eleven who live with white, single mothers
    d. girls between ages ten and thirteen who live with Hispanic, single fathers

13. _____ Mothers and children make up _____ percent of the homeless population.
    a. 20
    b. 30
    c. 40
    d. 50

14. _____ The federal Aid to Families with Dependent Children (AFDC) program ended in 1997, and a different federal program, _____, ensued.
    a. Welfare Reform for Families (WRF)
    b. Temporary Assistance for Needy Families (TANF)
    c. Modified Aid to Needy Families (MANF)
    d. Personal Responsibility and Work Opportunity (PRWO)

15. _____ Nearly _____ percent of all children have no health insurance, either public or private.
    a. 11
    b. 18
    c. 21
    d. 26

16. _____ The parenting style of adolescent mothers that encourages preschoolers to adjust well to school is the _____ style.
    a. authoritative
    b. laissez-faire
    c. authoritarian
    d. egalitarian

17. _____ In the United States, which of the following social strata have the money to fit the idealized cultural image of the self-sufficient nuclear family?
    a. the upper class
    b. the middle class
    c. the lower-middle class
    d. all of the above

18. _____ When parents place too many demands on children by engaging them in all sorts of lessons and activities, they are creating a _____ child.
    a. scheduled
    b. stressed
    c. hurried
    d. busy

19. _____ The text points out that, today, a majority of African Americans are members of the
_____ class.
   a. working or middle
   b. lower
   c. middle
   d. upper

20. _____ Native American parents have been described as exercising which parenting style?
   a. authoritarian
   b. authoritative
   c. laissez-faire
   d. egalitarian

21. _____ Compared to the average of slightly over 25 percent for all Americans over twenty-four
years old, _____ percent of Asians have completed four years of college or more.
   a. 30
   b. 35
   c. 40
   d. 45

22. _____ Which of the following is NOT one of the tips mentioned in the text for parents
who are rearing multiracial children?
   a. Encourage children to be proud of all their racial background.
   b. Understand that racial identity is fluid during adolescence.
   c. Avoid excessive praise, which could lead to false expectations.
   d. Stress the positives.

23. _____ Which of the following is NOT one of the three newly visible parenting
environments discussed in the text?
   a. gay and lesbian parents
   b. sharing parents
   c. grandparent parents
   d. foster parents

24. _____ More than _____ million children under age eighteen are living in a
grandparent's household.
   a. 0.6
   b. 1.6
   c. 2.6
   d. 3.6

25. _____ Some foster care takes place in _____, where several children are cared for round-
the-clock by paid professionals who work in shifts and live elsewhere.
   a. group homes
   b. agency centers
   c. day-care centers
   d. pre-schools

26. _____ Instead of punishing children, the text suggests all of the following EXCEPT
     a.   express your feeling strongly without attacking character.
     b.   state your expectations.
     c.   tell the child that they did something bad and they are bad.
     d.   give the child a choice.

27. _____ The person who is an unrelated adult who informally plays the role of a parent for a child is a
     a.   surrogate parent.
     b.   substitute parent.
     c.   part time parent.
     d.   para-parent.

28. _____ Parenting in Hispanic families that combines warm emotional support and a demand for significant respect for parents and other authority figures is
     a.   la familia importante.
     b.   hierarchical parenting.
     c.   authoritative parenting.
     d.   authoritarian parenting.

29. _____ Grandparents who are raising their grandchildren as children are characterized by all of the following EXCEPT
     a.   younger at the time of the birth of their first child.
     b.   female.
     c.   poor.
     d.   Asian American.

30. _____ When adult children return to their parents' home to live, the parents should
     a.   not charge rent.
     b.   set the rules.
     c.   require cleanliness.
     d.   set limits on noise levels.

TRUE-FALSE

1. _____ The text points out that parenting today takes place in a social context that can make child rearing an enormously difficult task.

2. _____ When a new mother's expectations about how much the father will be involved with the baby are met, the transition to parenthood is easier.

3. _____ Fathers typically engage in more hands-on parenting and take primary responsibility for children.

4. _____ Single, but not married, fathers who are primary parents report facing isolation and stereotypes.

5. _____ Generally, research shows that shared parenting increases children's behavior problems.

6. _____ Authoritative parents tend to have children who are socially competent and successful, with high self-esteem and cooperative, yet independent, personalities.

7. _____   Pediatricians and social scientists generally agree about the appropriateness of spanking.

8. _____   Research shows that spanking is usually more effective than timeouts.

9. _____   The hope that research in child development offers to parents who make mistakes is that children can be surprisingly resilient.

10. _____   The working full-time minimum wage does not provide a parent enough money to live above the poverty line.

11. _____   Despite higher rates of non-Hispanic white poverty, in sheer numbers, there are more white families in poverty.

12. _____   The rate of children's poverty in the United States is below that of the nation as a whole.

13. _____   Upper-middle-class parents can reasonably assume that their children will eventually enjoy positions in the upper-middle class.

14. _____   Parents usually agree on the best approach to racial issues.

15. _____   Individuals who have grandchildren living in their homes are almost always primary parents.

SHORT ANSWER

1.   What are the challenges facing grandparents as parents?

2.   What is *shared parenting*? Give an example.

3. How are never-married single mothers "different" from divorced, widowed, or separated mothers?

4. Based on the text's discussion, address the question, "Is spanking ever appropriate?"

5. In what way(s) are some children "resilient"? Give supportive information and/or research results as part of your answer.

ESSAY

1. Based on the text's discussion, describe the "transition to parenthood."

2. Explain Diana Baumrind's typology of the different types of parenting. Give an example of each.

3. What are the primary differences in parenting practice based on social class differences?

4. Compare and contrast African American, Native American, Hispanic, and Asian American parenting.

5. The text discusses three newly visible parenting environments. Identify and briefly discuss each one.

ANSWERS TO SAMPLE QUESTIONS

Completion (using key terms)

1.	foster	8.	Temporary Assistance for Needy Families
2.	grandparent	9.	Hierarchical
3.	Primary	10.	Confucian training
4.	parenting	11.	group
5.	authoritarian	12.	Family foster care
6.	laissez-faire	13.	Formal kinship care
7.	authoritative		

Multiple Choice (page references in parentheses)

1.	c (285)	16.	c (278)
2.	c (268)	17.	a (279)
3.	a (268)	18.	c (279)
4.	a (270)	19.	a (280)
5.	b (271)	20.	c (281)
6.	c (272)	21.	d (282)
7.	b (272)	22.	c (282-283)
8.	a (274)	23.	b (286-287)
9.	c (274)	24.	d (285)
10.	d (274)	25.	a (286)
11.	b (276)	26.	c (275)
12.	c (276)	27.	d (277)
13.	d (279)	28.	b (281)
14.	b (278)	29.	d (285)
15.	a (278)	30.	b (288)

True-False (answers in parentheses)

1.	T (266)	9.	T (277)
2.	T (270)	10.	F (278)
3.	F (271)	11.	T (281)
4.	F (271)	12.	F (278)
5.	F (272)	13.	F (279)
6.	T (273)	14.	F (284)
7.	F (276)	15.	F (285)
8.	F (276)		

CHAPTER 12

WORK AND FAMILY

CHAPTER SUMMARY

This chapter explores ways in which society has, through the invention of the postindustrial **labor force**, brought about dramatic changes in the traditional model of provider husbands and homemaking wives, producing both new options, along with a variety of rewards and costs.

The traditional model of provider husbands and homemaking wives has been replaced by a variety of alternatives, including the **main/secondary provider** couple, the **co-provider** couple, the **ambivalent provider** couple, the **role-reversed provider** couple, and the **househusbands**.

Women's participation in the labor force has increased greatly since the beginning of the nineteenth century; this trend accelerated during World War I and the Great Depression, and then expanding during the 1970s. The pronounced tendency for men and women to be employed in different types of jobs is termed **occupational** segregation. The **wage gap** varies by race and ethnicity. The concept **motherhood penalty** describes the fact that motherhood has a tremendous negative lifetime impact on earnings.

A large proportion of women in the labor force as paid workers has produced a wide variety of alternatives: **two-earner marriages two-career marriages**, self-employment vs. part-time employment, **shift work**, as well as the phenomenon of persons leaving the labor force and then returning to it (**sequencing moms**). The chapter distinguishes between **two-earner** and **two-career marriages**. In the latter, wives and husbands both earn high wages and work for intrinsic rewards. Even such marriages, the husband's career usually has priority. Responsibility for household work falls largely on wives. Many wives would prefer shared roles, and negotiation and tension over this issue casts a shadow on many marriages. An incomplete transition to equality at work and at home affects family life profoundly. The unexplored, unresolved issue of **unpaid family work** or housework has been brought abruptly to conscious consideration as a social issue. Sociologist Arlie Hochschild refers to what she calls the **second shift** of unpaid family work that amounts to an extra month of work each year for many employed wives. Hochschild refers to the fact that women are more likely to adjust their schedules to suit those of men as a **stalled revolution**.

Working people are spending significantly more hours at work, which has led to the juggling of employment and a hectic and stressful situation for many two-earner relationships. Children, as well as parents, are affected by this "juggling." This process is even more pronounced in two-career marriages. A career move for one spouse may make the other a **trailing** spouse who relocates to accommodate the other one's career. Social scientists have called marriages in which spouses live apart **commuter** marriages

The chapter emphasizes that both cultural expectations and public policy affect people's options. Most policy makers agree that single-parent and two-earner families are in need of more adequate provisions for **child care** and elder care. As individuals come to realize this, we can expect pressure on public officials to meet the needs of working families by providing supportive policies, **family leave**, and **flexible scheduling**, such as **job sharing** and **flextime**. Some large corporations demonstrate interest in effecting **family-friendly workplace policies** that are supportive of employee efforts to combine family and work commitments.

Household work and child care are pressure points as women enter the labor force and the two-earner marriage becomes the norm. How a couple allocates paid and unpaid work represents a combination of each partner's **gender strategy**. To make it work, either the structure of work must be changed, social policy must support working families, or women and men must change their household role patterns – and very probably all three.

LEARNING OBJECTIVES

Based on your careful and thorough reading of Chapter 12, you should:

1.   be familiar with the characteristics of the labor force in postindustrial society.

2.   be familiar with the traditional model of *provider husbands* and *homemaking wives.*

3.   understand the position of women in the labor force and the significance of the wage gap.

4.   be acquainted with how two-earner marriages have produced new work settings and provider-caregiving options.

5.   understand how contemporary women juggle employment and continue to assume most of the responsibility for unpaid family work.

6.   the impact of dual-income and dual-career families on people's health.

7.   be familiar with the text's discussion of what kinds of social policy are needed to resolve work-family issues.

8.   be acquainted with the controversy over child care

9.   understand the implications for two-earner marriages of maintaining intimacy while negotiating provider roles and the "second shift."

KEY TERMS (page references in parentheses)

attachment (318)
center care (317)
child care (316)
commuter marriage (316)
elder care (319)
family child care (317)
family-friendly workplace policy (322)
flexible scheduling (322)
flextime (322)
good provider role (300)
househusband (301)
in-home caregiver (317)
job sharing (322)
labor force (294)
market approach to child care (317)
motherhood penalty (297)
mothering approach to child care (316)

nanny (302)
neotraditional family (298)
occupational segregation (295)
opting out (298)
parenting approach to child care (317)
reinforcing cycle (307)
second shift (354)
self-care (307)
sequencing mom (306)
shift work (303)
stay-at-home dad (301)
trailing spouse (316)
two-career marriage (302)
two-earner marriage (348)
unpaid family work (306)
wage gap (296)

COMPLETION (using key terms)

1. What sociologist Jessie Bernard terms the _____ role for men emerged in the United States during the 1830s.

2. _____ are men who stay home to care for the house and family while their wives work.

3. Among some business, professional, and political families, wives are expected to help their husbands professionally by cultivating appropriate acquaintances and by being charming hostesses and companions. These wives are part of a _____ career.

4. The pronounced tendency for men and women to be employed in different types of jobs is termed _____.

5. _____ represents an active, affective, enduring, and reciprocal bond between two individuals that is believed to be established through repeated interaction over time.

6. Today, _____ marriages, in which both partners are in the labor force, are the statistical norm among married couples.

7. _____ work involves the necessary tasks of attending both the emotional needs of all family members and the practical needs of dependent members, as well as maintaining the family domicile.

8. The concept _____ describes the fact that motherhood has a tremendous negative lifetime impact on earnings.

9. Drawn from symbolic interaction theory and the ideological perspective, the _____ perspective looks to the *meaning* of housework, rather than the practicalities of time and income, to explain a gendered division of labor.

10. The _____ is the difference in earnings between men and women.

11. Policy researchers define _____ as the full-time care and education of children under age six, care before and after school and during school vacations for older children, and overnight care when employed parents must travel.

12. The term _____ refers to care provided in a caregiver's home, often by an older woman or a mother who has chosen to remain out of the labor force to care for her own children.

13. _____ involves an employee being able to take an extended period of time from work, either paid or unpaid, for the purpose of caring for a newborn, for a newly adopted or seriously ill child, for the care of an elderly parent, or for their own health needs with the guarantee of a job upon returning.

14. Job sharing and flextime are both examples of _____.

15. Some large corporations demonstrate interest in effecting _____ policies that are supportive of employee efforts to combine family and work commitments.

KEY THEORETICAL PERSPECTIVES

rational investment perspective
resource hypothesis
ideological perspective
gender construction perspective

INTERNET AND INFOTRAC EXERCISES

Internet Exercises

1.   The text discusses the wage gap between men and women in American society. For a detailed consideration of this issue and also a history of the legislation designed to produce pay equity, go to http://www.liwomen.com/payequity2.htm. After you have read the contents of this site, consider these questions:
   - Historically, what has been the justification for men being paid more than women in the labor force?
   - Do you think that *pay equity* legislation will put an end to the wage gap? Why or why not?
   - Do you support *comparable worth*? Why or why not?

2.   The following website offers an analysis of the challenges of shift work, including relationships with other family members: http://www.sleepdoctor.com/shift.htm. After you have read the article, respond to the following questions:
   - What are the challenges of shift work for the human body?
   - How is shift work in contradiction to the normal sleep cycle of human beings?
   - How can the suggestions made in this article be helpful to family members in reference to their relationships with each other?

3.   Arlie Hochschild and the *second shift* have become inextricably intertwined. In 1997, Ms. Hochschild participated in an interview on Public Broadcasting Stations nationwide. For excerpts from that interview, go to http://www.pbs.org/newshour/authors_corner/july-dec97/hoch4.html. After you have read the contents of this site, respond to the following questions:
   - Among twin-income and dual-career families, do you think there will *ever* be an equal sharing of household work? Why or why not?
   - There has been some indication that women *voluntarily* assume a larger share of household responsibilities because they feel that their male partners do not perform these tasks satisfactorily. How do you think this observation fits in with the sharing of housework?

4.   Read the article about commuter marriages at http://family.jrank.org/pages/296/Commuter-Marriages.html to learn more about why some couples opt for this arrangement. At the end of the article, click on the links and read about the demographics, benefits and challenges of living in a commuter marriage.
   - Do you think a commuter marriage is a healthy arrangement?
   - In many cases the income justifies the commuter marriage. Applying exchange theory to the concept of commuter marriages, do you think the benefits outweigh the costs? What are the costs? What are the benefits?

InfoTrac Exercises

1.   Use the key words *women in the labor force*. From the resulting list, select articles that focus on the contemporary status of women in the labor force, including nations other than the United States. After you have examined these articles, respond to the following questions:
   - How has the status of women in America's labor force improved over the years? Do you think there is room for more improvement? How?
   - How does the position of women in America's labor force compare with women in other nations?
   - Do you think that women will ever achieve *comparable worth* (that is, the wage gap will disappear)? Why or why not?

2.   Use the key words *dual-career marriage, a system in transition*. Read the review of the book by the same name, written by Lisa R. Silberstein. After you have read Deborah Arfkin's review, respond to the following questions:
   - What are Silberstein's major findings concerning dual-career marriages?
   - Would you consider a dual-career marriage? Why or why not?

3.   Use the key words *day care debate*. The controversy continues regarding the impact of day care on children. Given that the twin-income family is the norm today, an increasing proportion of children will spend time in child-care environments other than with parents in the home. After you have examined the articles available, consider the following questions:
   - Do you have a personal opinion about day care? What is it? How does your point of view align with existing research?
   - How do you see the future in reference to child care?

TRUE-FALSE

1. _____   According to the text, the labor force is a social invention.

2. _____   The good-provider role entailed only rewards, and no costs, for men.

3. _____   There is some evidence that there are distinct *good provider* and *involved father* models for a working man's response to parenthood.

4. _____   As late as 1940, only 14 percent of married women were in the labor force.

5. _____   Presently, homemaking is formal employment.

6. _____   Beginning in about 1960, the number of employed women began to increase rapidly.

7. _____   African American women have historically been less likely to work for wages in comparison with white women.

8. _____   The wage gap varies considerably depending on occupation, and tends to be greater in the more elite, higher-paying occupations.

9. _____   Home-based work has never involved what is referred to as *piecework*.

10. _____   Despite changing attitudes among couples and media portrayals of two-earner couples who share housework, women in fact continue to do more of it.

11. _____ A traditional division o labor is the ideal in neotraditional families..

12. _____ An American Time Use Survey conducted in 2003 revealed that, on average, employed women spent over two hours on household activities.

13. _____ Generally speaking, researchers conclude that commuter marriages have few rewards and many costs.

14. _____ With regard to mother-child interaction, child care exhibits a negative relationship to maternal sensitivity.

15. _____ According to the text's discussion, some staff turnover in child-care facilities is inevitable, but it should not exceed 25 percent a year.

MULTIPLE CHOICE

1. _____ Gradually throughout the twentieth century, American society moved from an industrial economic base that manufactured products to a postindustrial configuration that
   a. transmits information and offers other services.
   b. focuses only on profits.
   c. emphasizes aerospace industries.
   d. is most concerned with global commerce.

2. _____ The dramatic rise in women's employment began in the _____.
   a. 1940s
   b. 1950s
   c. 1960s
   d. 1970s

3. _____ Sociologist Jessie Bernard points out that, effective in the 1980 U.S. Census, a male was no longer automatically assumed to be head of the household. For Bernard, this marked the end of
   a. blatant sexism.
   b. the good provider role.
   c. sex discrimination.
   d. sexual harassment.

4. _____ In the majority of two-earner marriages, work-family arrangements are
   a. still the primary responsibility of the mother.
   b. accomplished by hiring a nanny.
   c. handled by both parents.
   d. determined by shifts.

5. _____ For two earner couples the tendency is for each to be employed in different types of jobs. This is termed
a.   market work.
b.   occupational separation.
c.   occupational segregation.
d.   shift work.

6. _____ In 2005, _____ percent of women worked part-time in the labor force.
a.   45
b.   35
c.   25
d.   15

7. _____ Currently, _____ of mothers with pre-school children worked full-time in 2004.
a.   more than one-third
b.   fewer than half
c.   two-thirds
d.   three-fourths

8. _____ The fact that motherhood has a tremendous life-time impact on earnings is the
a.   wage gap.
b.   motherhood penalty.
c.   career gap.
d.   income gap.

9. _____ In 2005, _____ percent of wives with children under age six were paid employees.
a.   20
b.   30
c.   40
d.   60

10. _____ The median annual earnings of male physicians in the United States is $144,000, compared to _____ for female physicians.
a. $68,000
b. $88,000
c. $108,000
d. $128,000

11. _____ In 1968, regarding the proportions of dual-earner and provider-housewife couples, there were
a.   more provider-housewife couples.
b.   more dual-earner couples.
c.   fewer of either of these categories in comparison with male-provider couples.
d.   equal proportions of each.

12. _____ All of the following account for the difference between earnings of men and women EXCEPT
a.   not ever working outside the home.
b.   fewer years of experience.
c.   not working full time.
d.   leaving the labor force for longer periods of time.

13. _____   In her job, Janet works five days a week, between the hours of 3 P.M. and 11 P.M. Janet's job may be classified as
   a.   shift work.
   b.   working class.
   c.   lower-middle class.
   d.   part-time work.

14. _____   In 1999, _____ percent of the labor force was self-employed.
   a.   2
   b.   4
   c.   6
   d.   8

15. _____   Janet is a mother who has chosen to leave her job as an accountant in order to spend some years at home raising children. Janet may be referred to as a(n) "_____ mom".
   a.   compartmentalizing
   b.   stay-at-home
   c.   sequencing
   d.   second-shift

16. _____   The text points out that American culture designates women as "_____," whose job it is to keep in touch with—and, if necessary, care for—adult siblings and other relatives.
   a.   housekeepers
   b.   homemakers
   c.   kinkeepers
   d.   professional domestics

17. _____   Among two-earner couples who share housework, the bulk of the work is
   a.   done by women.
   b.   done by men.
   c.   shared more or less equally.
   d.   necessarily shared.

18. _____   Marriage increases household labor hours for
   a.   both men and women.
   b.   women, but not for men.
   c.   men, but not for women.
   d.   men who do not work full-time.

19. _____   Women continue to feel responsible for family members' well-being and are more likely than men to adjust their work and home schedules to accommodate others. Arlie Hochschild calls this situation a(n)
   a.   second shift.
   b.   economic necessity.
   c.   stalled revolution.
   d.   conjugal paradox.

20. _____ The _____ suggests that one spouse's household labor is a consequence of her or his resources compared to those of the other.
   a. rational investment perspective
   b. ideological perspective
   c. functionalist perspective
   d. resource hypothesis

21. _____ Recent research suggests that in terms of reaching gender parity in the sharing of household work, most Americans judge their divisions of labor to be
   a. inequitable.
   b. unfair.
   c. fair.
   d. both a and b above

22. _____ The American Time Use Survey shows that women spend _____ percent more time than men in the care of the household and its members.
   a. 45
   b. 55
   c. 65
   d. 75

23. _____ _____ seem to have more difficulties with commuter marriages.
   a. Couples who have been married for shorter periods of time
   b. Couples who have been married for longer periods of time
   c. Women who have been single for a long period of time prior to marriage.
   d. Men who have been single for a long period of time prior to marriage.

24. _____ In the _____ approach, career-oriented couples hired other people to care for their children.
   a. parenting
   b. mothering
   c. market
   d. family child-care

25. _____ The concept of family leave incorporates which of the following?
   a. maternity
   b. paternity
   c. elder-care leaves
   d. all of the above

26. _____ A career move for one spouse may make the other a _____ spouse.
   a. trailing
   b. unemployed
   c. dislocated
   d. commuter

27. _____ Which of the following approaches to child care is most often adopted by both labor force elites and blue-collar, lower income families?
   a. mothering
   b. parenting
   c. market
   d. family

28. _____ Women who had impressive careers and have left employment to enjoy raising their children are defined as
   a.   nanny replacements.
   b.   opting out.
   c.   favoring motherhood.
   d.   labor force dropouts.

29. _____ Which of the following religious groups would be least likely to be associated with a neotraditional family?
   a.   Mormons
   b.   evangelical Christians
   c.   traditional Catholics
   d.   Episcopalians

30. _____ According to the U. S. Bureau of Labor Statistics, in 2006 what percentage of full-time workers have flexible schedules?
   a.   17
   b.   28
   c.   39
   d.   40

SHORT ANSWER

1.   For husbands, what are the rewards and the costs of the "good provider role?"

2.   What is the "second shift?" Give an example.

3.   What are the current controversies regarding child care outside of the home?

4.   What is the "life course solution" to day care?

5.   Outline the principal pressures on parents today.

ESSAY

1.   Compare and contrast the work realities of husbands and of wives.

2.   When couples change from being one-earner couples to being two-earner couples, what are the positive and negative consequences?

3.   Cecelia and Andre are both fully employed professionals who intend to marry. They both intend to continue their professional careers. What do sociologists know about this situation that might be useful to Cecelia and Andre?

4.   Explain why only a small percentage of men decide to become "househusbands."

5.   Based on the text's discussion, how can couples maintain intimacy while negotiating provider roles and the "second shift?"

ANSWERS TO SAMPLE QUESTIONS

Completion (using key terms)

1. good provider
2. Househusbands
3. two-person single
4. occupational segregation
5. Attachment
6. two-earner
7. Unpaid family
8. motherhood penalty
9. gender construction
10. wage gap
11. child care
12. family child care
13. Family leave
14. flexible scheduling
15. family-friendly workplace

True-False (page references in parentheses)

1. T (294)
2. F (300)
3. T (301)
4. T (394)
5. F (298)
6. T (294)
7. F (298)
8. T (296)
9. F (303)
10. T (307)
11. T (298)
12. T (312)
13. F (316)
14. T (318)
15. T (320)

Multiple Choice (page references in parentheses)

1. a (294)
2. c (294)
3. b (300)
4. a (302)
5. d (295)
6. c (303)
7. b (303)
8. b (297)
9. d (295)
10. b (296)
11. d (302)
12. a (297)
13. a (303)
14. d (304)
15. c (306)
16. c (306)
17. a (307)
18. b (354-355)
19. c (307)
20. d (356)
21. c (480)
22. d (312)
23. a (316)
24. c (316)
25. d (322)
26. a (316)
27. b (316)
28. b (298)
29. d (298)
30. d (322)

CHAPTER 13

COMMUNICATION IN MARRIAGE AND FAMILIES

CHAPTER SUMMARY

Family cohesion refers to the emotional bonding of family members. Research makes it clear that the existence or nonexistence of positive feelings is a very important determinant of marital and family happiness. Nick Stinnett has identified a number of qualities that relate to family strengths: appreciation for one another, arranging personal schedules to do things together, a high degree of commitment, a spiritual orientation, dealing positively with crisis, and positive communication. Another important ingredient in an emotionally bonded relationship is to let your partner know you are listening. Active listening involves paying close attention to what the other person is saying, coupled with **giving feedback** and **checking-it-out**. Happy couples typically let each other know they are listening through the use of **listener backchannels**. Communication and couple satisfaction are necessarily linked.

Marital anger and conflict are necessary forces and a challenge to be met rather than avoided. Many married couples are reluctant to fight, and this reluctance can be destructive. There are a number of potential side effects of conflict avoidance, including **passive aggression** (**sabotage** and **displacement**), and the suppression of anger.

Social psychologist John Gottman has written extensively about marital communication. He refers to **The Four Horsemen of the Apocalypse: contempt, criticism, defensiveness**, and **stonewalling**. Later, he added **belligerence** to this list. Supportive communication is extremely important. There are key gender differences in couple communication. Deborah Tannen points out that men typically engage in **report talk**, while women are likely to engage in **rapport talk**. The **female-demand/male-withdraw pattern** can cause a great deal of difficulty in terms of couple communication. Gottman stresses that partners should try to be gentle and soothing toward one another and do what they can to encourage signs of affection. Avoiding or evading a fight is an example of stonewalling, which can lead to **gunnysacking**: keeping one's grievances secret.

Some goals and strategies can help make conflict management productive rather than destructive. This kind of fighting has been called **bonding fighting**. There are nine specific guidelines involved in this process: leveling with each other, using "I" statements when possible, avoiding mixed or double messages, choosing the time and place for grievances carefully, focusing anger only on specific issues, asking for a specific change but being open to compromise, being willing to change yourself, not trying to win, and remembering to end the argument.

Couples can strive to change their conflict management habits. Both generational and couple change are involved here. Learning to fight fair is not easy.

So much attention has been devoted to the bonding capacity of intimate fighting that it may seem as if conflict itself can be free of conflict, but this is a myth.

LEARNING OBJECTIVES

Based on your careful and thorough reading of Chapter 13, you should:

1.	be familiar with the dynamics of family cohesion, the importance of letting your partner know you are listening, and the concept of "active listening."

2.	be familiar with Nick Stinnett's six qualities of strong families.

3.	appreciate the relationship between communication and couple satisfaction.

4.	understand and appreciate the relationship between conflict and love and the liabilities associated with denying conflict.

5.	be familiar with the processes of supportive couple communication and conflict management.

6.	know about the Four Horsemen of the Apocalypse (and belligerence).

7.	understand the concept of "bonding fights" and the nine guidelines associated with this process.

8.	be familiar with the dynamics of changing fighting habits.

9.	understand the myth of conflict-free conflict.

KEY TERMS (page references in parentheses)

belligerence (338)
bonding fighting (342)
contempt (336)
criticism (336)
defensiveness (336)
displacement (336)
family cohesion (330)
female-demand/male-withdraw
	communication pattern (338)

Four Horsemen of the Apocalypse (336)
leveling (342)
listener backchannel (333)
mixed, or double, messages (343)
passive-aggression (335)
rapport talk (338)
report talk (338)
sabotage (336)
stonewalling (336

COMPLETION (using key terms)

1.	_____ refers to the emotional bonding of family members.

2.	In _____, one partner attempts to spoil or undermine some activity the other has planned.

3.	In _____, a person directs anger at people or things that the other cherishes.

4.	Contempt, criticism, defensiveness, and stonewalling are Gottman's _____.

5.	Rolling one's eyes indicates _____, a feeling that one's spouse is inferior or undesirable.

6. _____ involves making disapproving judgments or evaluations of one's partner.

7. _____ means preparing to defend oneself against what one presumes is an upcoming attack.

8. _____ is resistance, refusing to listen to one's partner, particularly to a partner's complaints.

9. _____ is a behavior that is provocative and that challenges the spouse's power and authority.

10. Deborah Tannen argues that men typically engage in _____ talk.

11. Deborah Tannen argues that women typically engage in _____ talk.

12. _____ refers to keeping one's grievances secret while tossing them into an imaginary location.

13. When _____, a partner repeats in her or his own words what the other has said or revealed.

14. _____ involves asking the other person whether your perception of his or her feelings or of the present situation is accurate.

15. _____ messages are simultaneous messages that contradict each other.

KEY THEORETICAL PERSPECTIVES

the conflict perspective on love
Gottman's Four Horsemen of the Apocalypse (conflict theory)

INTERNET AND INFOTRAC EXERCISES

Internet Exercises

1. The Internet is filled with sites and resources that relate to *couple communication*, such as http://www.couplecommunication.com/. When you reach the main page, review the programs for developing effective communication skills within intimate relationship(s). After you have completed this exploration, respond to the following questions:
   • Using the text and this website as resources, make a list of the most important ingredients of effective couple communication.
   • After you have completed this list, evaluate your own intimate relationship experience(s) utilizing these principles. Are you able to identify certain areas where your own communication skills could use some improvement? If so, what specifically do you think you can improve upon?

2. The text discusses supportive couple communication and conflict management. There are many sites on the Internet that deal with these topics. One location is the Florida Marriage Preparation Series. Go to http://edis.ifas.ufl.edu/BODY_FY047. From the main page, click on the icon to view the entire publication, "Conflict Management and Resolution: Can We Agree?" You will need Adobe Acrobat in order to read the article; this software is available through the Internet and

should not be hard to download, if it is not already resident in the computer you are using. The article is not long, so it shouldn't take you that long to read it in its entirety. After you have read the article, respond to these questions:

- The article lists *positive* and *negative aspects of conflict*. Compare and contrast this discussion with the text's treatment of "supportive communication" and the nine guidelines for "bonding fights." What are the similarities between these discussions?
- The article identifies five basic steps to problem solving. In your own intimate relationship(s), do you employ these basic steps? In what ways do you think you can improve your communication skills by managing conflict more effectively?

3.   Go to http://raysweb.net/poems/articles/tannen.html. Read the excerpt, "Can't We Talk" that has been drawn from Deborah Tannen's book, *You Just Don't Understand*. After you have examined Tannen's observations, respond to the following questions:
- What is the fundamental difference between
    a.   "status" and "support"
    b.   "independence" and "intimacy"
    c.   "advice" and "understanding"
    d.   "information" and "feelings"
    e.   "orders" and "proposals"
    f.   "conflict" and "compromise"?

4.   The text discusses the benefits of letting your partner know you are listening and the importance of "active listening" in intimate relationships. Essentially, good communication is the key to good relationships, and listening is essential for effective communication. Are you willing to test your listening skills? Go to: http://www.positive-way.com/listenin.htm. The "listening quiz" is presented so that you *and* a partner can participate together but, if this isn't feasible, you can respond to the inventory by yourself. After you have completed the quiz, click on *rating discussion and listening advice*. This will provide an interpretation of your score on the quiz. After you have read this material, respond to these questions:
- Are you surprised by your "score" on the listening quiz? Why or why not?
- If you participated with a partner, how did the two of you compare? Do you think that the "listening quiz" revealed anything about your relationship that you did not already know? If so, what?
- Do you think you can improve upon your listening skills? After reading Chapter 13, are you any more confident that relationship success is linked to listening skills and effective communication? Why or why not?

5.   Many families have difficulty in talking to their teenage children. Go to http://www.familycommunication.org/ and read some of the suggestions about talking to teenagers Can you remember some of the difficulties you may have had in communicating with your parents when you were a teen?
- After reading these suggestions, evaluate the suggestions. Do you have other suggestions to offer?

InfoTrac Exercises

1.   Use the keywords *the key to family cohesion: finding time to eat together*. Read the article drawn from *The Philadelphia Inquirer* by Jane Eisner, then respond to these questions:
- Why does Eisner think it is so important for family members to eat together?
- Think about your own family experiences. Do the members of your family "find time to eat together?" Do you agree that this is important? Why or why not?

2. Use the keyword *conflict management*. Focus on those articles that deal with managing conflict within intimate/personal relationships. Depending upon how much time you have, read one or two of the articles that appear most interesting to you. Then, respond to these questions:
   - The text points out that "supporting couple communication" is extremely important in reference to conflict management. Did the article(s) you read confirm this connection in some way? How?
   - One of the articles listed by InfoTrac is authored by social psychologist John Gottman ("Psychology and the Study of Marital Processes"). Whether or not this is one of the articles you selected, Gottman's research and his "Four Horsemen of the Apocalypse": contempt, criticism, defensiveness, and stonewalling, are discussed in the text. Using the text's discussion and what you learned from the article(s) you read in this exercise, why are these four variables so important in reference to communication in relationships?

3. Use the keywords *communication in marriage*. Select several articles and take a closer look at them. Respond to the following questions:
   - What is unique about marital communication? Any intimate relationship depends on effective communication for its success, but marriage usually implies constant contact between partners. When people are together a great deal, and when the definition of their relationship includes intimacy and closeness, why is communication such a critical variable?
   - The text discusses "the myth of the conflict-free conflict." How do the observations surrounding this discussion relate to marital communication? What did you learn from the articles you read that help to better understand the relationship between marital communication and marital conflict?

MULTIPLE CHOICE

1. _____ One way to look at couple communication and satisfaction is through the _____ perspective, whereby family interaction is seen as influenced by outside stressors, such as economic recession or racism.
   a. interactionist
   b. ecology
   c. functionalist
   d. conflict

2. _____ The text points out that Chapter 13 focuses on couple communication using mainly a(n) _____ perspective.
   a. conflict
   b. functionalist
   c. ecology
   d. interactionist

3. _____ The emotional bonding of family members is referred to as family
   a. strength.
   b. construction.
   c. cohesion.
   d. justice.

4. _____ Which of the following is NOT one of Nick Stinnett's qualities that reflect family strengths?
   a. appreciation for one another
   b. spiritual orientation
   c. dealing positively with crisis
   d. negative affect

5. _____ Which of the following is NOT one of Carlfred Broderick's positive results of good listening?
   a. learning how to use negative affect
   b. setting an example for your spouse to follow in listening to your feelings
   c. discovering how things actually look from your spouse's or partner's point of view
   d. avoiding interrupting and criticizing

6. _____ Fitzpatrick's research uncovered "_____ couples": spouses who have dissimilar ideologies of marriage and differ in their expectations for closeness and attitudes toward conflict.
   a. misdirected
   b. divergent
   c. mixed
   d. negative affect

7. _____ When a person expresses anger at someone but does so indirectly rather than directly, that behavior is called
   a. authoritarianism.
   b. displacement.
   c. sabotage.
   d. passive-aggression.

8. _____ Which of the following is NOT one of the "rules for a successful relationship," as discussed in the text?
   a. Be willing to challenge your partner's demands and question his/her shortcomings.
   b. Share more about yourself with your partner than you do with any other person.
   c. Express your love materially.
   d. Do not take your relationship for granted.

9. _____ The text points out that people use passive-aggression for the same reason they use anger substitutes – they are
   a. looking for a peaceful solution to conflict.
   b. trying to be cooperative.
   c. afraid of direct conflict.
   d. bored.

10. _____ Stephanie is angry with her husband for spending what she thinks is too much time on his career, and she expresses hatred for his expensive automobile. Stephanie's behavior reflects
   a. sabotage.
   b. displacement.
   c. suppression of anger.
   d. martyrdom.

11. _____ In the 1970s, social psychologist John Gottman applied a(n) _____ perspective to partner communication, and began studying newly married couples.
    a. functionalist
    b. conflict
    c. ecological
    d. interactionist

12. _____ *Contempt, criticism, defensiveness,* and *stonewalling* are all examples of what social psychologist John Gottman referred to as the
    a. Four Horsemen of the Apocalypse.
    b. major threats to communication breakdown.
    c. Four Riders of the Communication Barrier.
    d. primary ingredients of impending divorce.

13. _____ John Gottman and his colleagues observed that marriages will work to the extent that they provide for *soothing of the male*. By this, these researchers were referring to things people do to
    a. support the male ego.
    b. avoid conflict.
    c. reduce physical stress symptoms.
    d. calm emotional reactions.

14. _____ Which of the following is NOT one of the general conclusions of John Gottman's research on marital communication and conflict management?
    a. Both partners need to do what they can to de-escalate arguments.
    b. Partners can learn self-soothing techniques.
    c. Partners, especially husbands, need to be willing to accept influence from their wives.
    d. Both partners need to be willing to challenge each other's demands.

15. _____ Fight evaders use several tactics to avoid fighting. Which of the following is NOT one of these?
    a. derailing potential arguments by saying "I *will not* tolerate your yelling at me."
    b. by flatly stating, "I can't take you seriously when you act this way."
    c. by using the "hit and run" tactic of filing a complaint, then leaving no time for an answer or for a resolution
    d. by turning sullen and refusing to argue or talk

16. _____ Marilyn has many grievances about her husband's behavior, but she has kept these accumulating thoughts secret for a long time. Marilyn's approach reflects
    a. sabotage.
    b. gunnysacking.
    c. refusing to accept influence.
    d. negative affect.

17. _____ The text observes that *leveling* is which of the following in action?
    a. gunnysacking
    b. refusing to accept influence
    c. self-disclosure
    d. sabotage

18. _____ The text observes that the first step in improving one's marital communication is to
   a. fight fairly.
   b. over a long period of time.
   c. gracefully.
   d. have realistic expectations.

19. _____ Because partners who are just learning to manage their conflicts constructively may be anxious or insecure, the text recommends which of the following as a way to begin?
   a. write letters or use a tape recorder
   b. arrange for an up-front confrontation
   c. achieve face-to-face communication immediately
   d. avoid bonding fighting

20. _____ A study comparing mutually satisfied couples with those experiencing marital difficulties found that when couples are having trouble getting along or are stressed, they tend to interpret each other's messages and behavior
   a. much more positively.
   b. somewhat more positively.
   c. more negatively.
   d. as absolutely negative, with no exceptions.

21. _____ The verbal or nonverbal expressions of one's feelings of affection toward another is
   a. positive action
   b. positive benefit
   c. positive affect
   d. positive effect

22. _____ Which of the following is not an example of a listener backchannel?
   a. brief vocalization
   b. forgetting important events
   c. nagging
   d. procrastination

23. _____ When one partner attempts to undermine some activity the other has planned, this is known as
   a. displacement.
   b. stonewalling.
   c. defensiveness.
   d. sabotage.

24. _____ Gottman later added a fifth element of conflict and anger. What is that element?
   a. defensiveness
   b. belligerence
   c. contempt
   d. criticism

25. _____ The common communication pattern between partners occurs so often that therapists have named it
   a. female report/male rapport.
   b. male demand/female withdraw.
   c. female demand/male withdraw.
   d. female passive/male aggressive.

26. _____ All of the following are examples of passive-aggression EXCEPT
    a.   chronic criticism.
    b.   forgetting important events.
    c.   nagging.
    d.   procrastination.

27. _____ Fighting that brings couples closer together is
    a.   marriage strengthening.
    b.   bonding.
    c.   gunnysacking.
    d.   brownbagging.

28. _____ The first step in improving one's marital communication is to
    a.   get stuff done.
    b.   not put off major discussions.
    c.   recognize areas of disagreement.
    d.   set realistic expectations about the relationship.

29. _____ All of the following are examples of stonewalling EXCEPT
    a.   leaving the house when a fight threatens.
    b.   refusing to argue or talk.
    c.   being transparent.
    d.   saying "Okay, you win."

30. _____ Which of the following is NOT one of the signs that characterize an unhappy marriage according to John Gottman's research?
    a.   supportive communication
    b.   contempt
    c.   belligerence
    d.   defensiveness

TRUE-FALSE

1. _____ Conflict is a challenge to be avoided.

2. _____ Nick Stinnett found that members of strong families arranged their personal schedules so that they could do things, or simply be, together.

3. _____ Findings from a large national sample show that being religious necessarily makes for happier marriages.

4. _____ The first rule for a successful relationship is to express love verbally.

5. _____ Psychologists Nathaniel Branden and Robert Sternberg recommend that loving couples should practice the "golden rule."

6. _____ Early in his research, John Gottman concluded that wives and husbands have different goals when they disagree.

7. _____ Men typically engage in rapport talk..

8. _____ Leaving the house or the scene when a fight threatens is an example of stonewalling.

9. _____ A rule in avoiding attack is to use "I" statements rather than "you" or "why" statements.

10. _____ Bonding fights always involve a winner and a loser.

11. _____ Communication is a two-way process involving a sender and a receiver.

12. _____ Social scientist Suzanne Steinmetz's research shows not only that individual families assume consistent patterns or habits for facing conflict but that these patterns are passed from one generation to the next.

13. _____ The first step in changing destructive fighting habits is to record a fight and play it back later.

14. _____ When both partners develop constructive habits, all of their problems will be solved.

15. _____ All negative facts and feelings need to be communicated.

SHORT ANSWER

1. What is *family cohesion*? Give an example.

2. Explain the difference between "I-statements" and "leveling." Give an example of each.

3.   Distinguish between "report talk" and "rapport talk" as styles of communication. Give an example of each.

4.   What is "supportive communication?" Give several examples.

5.   What are "bonding fights?" Give an example

ESSAY

1.   List and briefly discuss Nick Stinnett's six qualities of "strong families."

2.   What are the likely results of denying conflict?

3.   Outline the major gender differences in couple communication.

4.   Identify the "Four Horsemen of the Apocalypse." Why are these elements so important to couple communication and conflict management? How does *belligerence* fit in here?

5.   What does it take for couples to change their fighting habits?

ANSWERS TO SAMPLE QUESTIONS

Completion (using key terms)

1. Family cohesion
2. sabotage
3. displacement
4. Four Horsemen of the Apocalypse
5. contempt
6. Criticism
7. Defensiveness
8. Stonewalling
9. Belligerence
10. report
11. rapport
12. Gunnysacking
13. giving feedback
14. Checking-it-out
15. Mixed or double

Multiple Choice (page references in parentheses)

1. b (330)
2. d (330)
3. c (330)
4. d (332)
5. a (333)
6. c (330)
7. d (335)
8. a (334)
9. c (335)
10. b (336)
11. d (336)
12. a (336)
13. c (340)
14. d (338)
15. a (343)
16. b (344)
17. c (346)
18. d (346)
19. a (346)
20. c (347)
21. c (331)
22. b (333)
23. d (336)
24. b (336-337)
25. c (338)
26. b (335)
27. b (342)
28. d (346)
29. c (341-342)
30. a (340)

True-False (page references in parentheses)

1. T (334)
2. T (332)
3. F (332)
4. T (334)
5. T (334)
6. T (336)
7. F (338)
8. F (341)
9. T (343)
10. F (342)
11. T (343)
12. T (345)
13. F (346)
14. F (347)
15. F (347)

CHAPTER 14

POWER AND VIOLENCE IN FAMILIES

CHAPTER SUMMARY

Power may be defined as the ability to exercise one's will. There are many kinds of power, including **personal**, **social**, and **marital power**.

Marital power is complex and consists of several components: decision making, a division of labor, and a sense of empowerment. There are **objective measures of power** and **subjective measures of fairness** in marriages. For the most part, research shows that it is partners' subjective perception of fairness (as opposed to objective measures of actual equality) that influences marital satisfaction. There are six bases or sources of power: **coercive, reward, expert, informational, referent,** and **legitimate**.

Blood and Wolfe reasoned in their **resource hypothesis**, that the spouse with more resources has more power in marriage. Blood and Wolfe's research had the important effect of encouraging people to see conjugal power as shared rather than patriarchal, but it has also been criticized. There are various criticisms of this explanation. Feminist Dair Gillespie pointed out that power-giving resources tend to be unevenly distributed between the sexes. In a traditional society, male authority is traditional power; this perspective is termed **resources in cultural** context. In sum, the cultural context conditions resource theory. Resource theory explains marital power only when there is no overriding **egalitarian norm** or **patriarchal norm** of marital power The **relative love and need theory** is a variation of exchange theory. The majority of Americans, regardless of social class, do not see power inequities in their own marriages, although they obviously exist in many marriages. Black couples report more egalitarian relationships than those in other racial/ethnic groups. "Black matriarchy" is a myth, and so may be the belief that Mexican Americans behave only according to patriarchal standards Korean married women are more subject to traditional male dominance and the resources in cultural context theory seems operative in Korean American families. The preponderance of the evidence indicates that men are more dominant in marital relationships, but this situation is changing in American society. Equalization of the marital power of men and women may occur in a number of different ways.

Sociologists Philip Blumstein and Pepper Schwartz undertook a comparison of four types of couples: heterosexual married couples, cohabiting heterosexual couples, gay male couples, and lesbian couples. These researchers found gender to be by far the most significant determinant of **intimate-partner power**. They found that commitment influences the use of power. Schwartz followed up on this research on four types of couples with an exploration of the factors that facilitate **peer marriage**. She found that couples' respect for each other is essentially a "no-power" relationship.

Current evidence indicates that equitable relationships are generally more apt to be stable and satisfying. Social scientist Peter Blau terms this situation **no-power**, which means that both partners wield about equal power. Consequently, they are able to avoid **power politics**. Both equal and unequal partners may engage in a cycle of devitalizing power politics. There are various alternative to this kind of power struggle. Unequal relationships discourage closeness between partners and communication is very important.

Physical violence is most commonly used in the absence of other resources. There are three major sources of data on family violence: the National Family Violence Surveys, the National Crime Victimization Survey, and the National Violence Against Women Survey. Although both men and women may abuse their spouses, women are significantly more likely than men to be victims of intimate-partner violence and the circumstances and outcomes of marital violence indicate that wife abuse is a more crucial social problem. It has received the most programmatic attention. Racial/ethnic comparisons are difficult to make. Recently, programs have been developed for male abusers, but less attention has been paid to male victims. Wife and female-partner abuse may take the form of sexual abuse and rape. The **three-phase cycle of** violence is helpful in understanding domestic abuse. Battered women's lack of personal power begins with fear. Among the variables involved with domestic violence are economic dependence, gendered socialization, childhood experiences, and low self-esteem. Shelters and domestic violence programs can be helpful. Research results have frequently been contradictory and the root explanation for these differences may be that there are two forms of heterosexual violence against women: **patriarchal** terrorism and **common couple** violence. Among the combative strategies are the shelter movement, counseling and group therapy directed toward abusive male partners, and the criminal justice system. Some studies indicate that mandatory arrest could be an important deterrent to future violence, but other investigations do not reach the same conclusion.

Economic hardships and concerns (among parents of all social classes and races) can lead to physical and/or emotional **child abuse** – a serious problem in our society and probably far more common than statistics indicate. One difficulty is drawing a clear distinction between "normal" childrearing and child abuse. There are other, related, problems, including **child neglect, emotional child abuse or neglect, sexual abuse, incest,** and **sibling violence**, the latter being the most pervasive form of family violence. There are various risk factors for child abuse. There are two major approaches to combating child abuse: the therapeutic approach and the criminal justice approach; the text adds a third: the social welfare approach.

LEARNING OBJECTIVES

Based on your careful and thorough reading of Chapter 14, you should:

1. be able to define power and be familiar with marital power and the different bases of power.

2. be familiar with the dynamics of marital power, including egalitarian power, the resource hypothesis, and the criticisms of the resource hypothesis.

3. be able to explain the relationship between resources and gender and resources in cultural context.

4. be familiar with the relationship between social class, racial/ethnic diversity, and marital power.

5. be familiar with Blumstein and Schwartz's typology of couples and their major research findings.

6. be familiar with peer marriage.

7. understand the relationship between power politics in marriage and no-power relationships, and the alternatives to power politics.

8. be familiar with the major sources of data on family violence.

9. understand the relationship between racial/ethnic diversity and abuse; the details on domestic violence among gay men, lesbians, and bisexual couples; and the relationship between immigration and family violence.

10. be familiar with wife and female partner abuse and with husband and male partner abuse.

11. be familiar with child abuse and neglect, including the risk factors for child abuse and the primary methods of combating child abuse.

KEY TERMS (page references in parentheses)

allocation systems (358)
child abuse (379)
child neglect (379
coercive power (353)
common couple violence (376)
Conflict Tactics Scale (367)
egalitarian norm [of
  marital power] (356)
emotional child abuse or
  neglect (380)
equality (352
equity (352)
expert power (353)
family preservation (383)
gender model of marriage (362)
incest (380)
informational power (353)
intimate partner power (352)
intimate-partner violence (367)
legitimate power (353)
marital power (352)
marital rape (370)

mutually economically dependent spouses
  [MEDS] (361)
near-peer marriage
  [Schwartz's typology] (370)
neotraditional family (361)
patriarchal norm [of
  marital power] (356)
patriarchal terrorism (376)
peer marriage
  [Schwartz's typology] (362)
power (352)
power politics (363)
referent power (353)
resource hypothesis (354)
resources in cultural context (355)
reward power (353)
sexual abuse (380)
sibling violence (380)
traditionals [Schwartz's
  typology] (362)
transitional egalitarian
  situation [of marital
  power] (355)

COMPLETION (using key terms)

1. _____ power refers to power in marriage.

2. _____ power is based on an individual's ability to give material or nonmaterial gifts and favors.

3. _____ power is based on the less dominant person's emotional identification with the more dominant individual.

4. If a(n) _____ norm of marriage were completely accepted, then a husband's superior economic achievements would be irrelevant to his decision-making power.

5. Like resource theory, the _____ theory is a variation of exchange theory.

6. _____ refers to overt acts of aggression toward children.

7. _____ refers to acts of omission toward children.

8. _____ refers to situations in which a child is forced, tricked, or coerced into sexual behavior.

9. _____ violence is the most pervasive form of family violence.

10. The _____ model views elder abuse and neglect as one form of family violence and focuses on characteristics of abusers and on situations that put potential victims at increased risk.

KEY THEORETICAL PERSPECTIVES

resource theory
family ecology perspective
relative love and need theory

INTERNET AND INFOTRAC EXERCISES

<u>Internet Exercises</u>

1. Child abuse is a particularly controversial area within the broader topic of family violence. Children are almost always seen as innocent victims and the reality of how many children are abused is shocking to most people. A very hazy area involves *emotional abuse*. Go to: http://www.safechild.org/childabuse3.htm. After you have read the contents, respond to the following questions:
   - What *is* emotional child abuse? Quite obviously, it is hard to recognize. Do you know a child who you suspect is a victim of emotional abuse? If so, what makes you think this youngster is a victim?
   - How does emotional child abuse occur? Do you think that most parents are *aware* that they are emotionally abusing their children?
   - What do you think is the solution to emotional child abuse?

2.   Marital rape is a controversial subject that is frequently misunderstood. In the first place, some traditionalists still emphasize the "right" of a husband to have sex with his wife whenever he chooses, since she is regarded as his "property." The state of Oregon has been a leader in terms of enacting laws concerning marital rape. Go to: http://www.mvwcs.com/maritalrape.html. There, you will find an interesting discussion of *marital and power rape*. After you have considered the discussion, respond to the following questions:
- What is a "power rapist?"
- Explain how "date rape" is a form of sexual assault.
- What does the victim of marital rape "need to know?"

3.   The *Stop Family Violence Organization* maintains an active site on the Internet: http://www.stopfamilyviolence.org/. From the main page, click on "family violence statistics." From that screen, click on "domestic violence statistics." The information in this section of the website should supplement your knowledge after having read Chapter 11. After you have familiarized yourself with these statistics, respond to the following questions:
- What is the relationship between *minority status* and family violence? In particular, how are *immigrants* affected?
- How does a woman's *pregnancy* affect her chances for being the victim of abuse?
- What category of women are the *most vulnerable* to abusive behavior?
- What suggestions do you have for solving the problem of domestic violence?

4.   Domestic violence extends to immigrant women. Go to http://endabuse.org/programs/display.php3?DocID=9927 and read about the efforts to prevent violence against immigrant women.
- How many immigrant women are victims of domestic violence?
- Why are immigrant women more likely to be victims of domestic violence?
- What programs are designed to help immigrant women?

InfoTrac Exercises

1.   Use the keywords *power politics in marriage*. You should find an article written by Erica Jong entitled "Hilary's Husband Reelected: The Clinton Marriage of Politics and Power." After you have read this article, respond to the following questions:
- Based on Jong's observations, how is *power* related to the marriage between Hilary and Bill Clinton?
- What were Hilary Clinton's *practical* motivations for her marriage to Bill Clinton? How does this reflect men's power in marriage situations?

2.   Use the keywords *perceived power and physical violence in marital conflict*. Read the article written by Sagrestano and her colleagues. Then, respond to the following questions:
- What are the primary findings of the research that these investigators conducted?
- What are your reactions to and/or criticisms of these findings?

3.   Use the keywords *explaining the recent decline in family violence*. Read the article written by Amy Farmer and Jill Tiefenthaler. Then, respond to the following questions:
- How do these authors explain the recent decline in family violence?
- Do you agree or disagree with Farmer and Tiefenthaler's interpretation? Why or why not?

MULTIPLE CHOICE

1. _____   Which type of power refers to the ability of people to exercise their wills over the wills of others?
   a.   personal
   b.   marital
   c.   social
   d.   objective

2. _____   In their relationship, Jacob *actually* makes more or more important decisions than his wife Kathy. This fact is a(n) _____ measure of power.
   a.   objective
   b.   subjective
   c.   egalitarian
   d.   marital

3. _____   Which of the following is NOT one of the bases, or sources, of power discussed in the text?
   a.   informational
   b.   referent
   c.   legitimate
   d.   sexual

4. _____   Samantha has convinced her husband Jack that he should stop smoking by giving him information on the health dangers associated with the habit. This illustrates which source of power?
   a.   coercive
   b.   informational
   c.   expert
   d.   referent

5. _____   John really doesn't want to go to the office party, but his wife Susan wants to, so he agrees to attend. This illustrates which source of power?
   a.   referent
   b.   legitimate
   c.   coercive
   d.   informational

6. _____   Rose and Randy have been married for several years. Both of them accept the traditional perception that Randy is the "head" of the family. This illustrates which source of power?
   a.   coercive
   b.   reward
   c.   expert
   d.   legitimate

7. _____   In their investigations involving the resource hypothesis, Blood and Wolfe came under the heaviest fire for their conclusion that
   a.   conjugal power is shared.
   b.   conjugal power is patriarchal.
   c.   a patriarchal power structure has been replaced by egalitarian marriages.
   d.   the resource hypothesis is too narrowly focused.

8. _____ In a traditional society, male authority is *legitimate power*. This observation is a reflection of which perspective?
   a. the principle of least interest
   b. resources in cultural context
   c. relative love and need theory
   d. referent power

9. _____ Which theory involves the point of view that each partner brings resources to the marriage and receives rewards from the other partner?
   a. resource
   b. the principle of least interest
   c. relative love and need
   d. conjugal power

10. _____ In Blumstein and Schwartz's investigations, which category of couples tended to be the *least* egalitarian?
    a. gay
    b. lesbian
    c. bisexual
    d. marital and cohabiting

11. _____ In the Blumstein and Schwartz study, which category of couples transcended the principle that economic resources determine decision-making power?
    a. lesbian
    b. gay
    c. marital
    d. cohabiting

12. _____ In Pepper Schwartz's investigation of 57 egalitarian couples and some additional interviews for comparison, _____ were those in which males dominated decision making except regarding children, but both parties were okay with this: The wife did not seek equality.
    a. near peers
    b. traditionals
    c. peers
    d. cohorts

13. _____ Social scientist Peter Blau refers to the situation where both partners wield about equal power as
    a. egalitarianism.
    b. no-power.
    c. shared power.
    d. equalitarianism.

14. _____ In addressing family violence, the text assumes that all forms of abuse have at their center
    a. the exploitation of a power difference.
    b. money issues.
    c. sexual issues.
    d. love issues.

15. _____   According to the National Crime Victimization Survey, there were over _____ incidents of victimization between intimates in 2004.
    a.   10,000
    b.   100,000
    c.   250,000
    d.   600,000

16. _____   In discussing gender and racial differences as to the decline in the numbers of intimate partner homicides, the text observes that *rates* of homicide victimization remain
    a.   much lower for blacks than for whites.
    b.   much lower for Hispanics than for whites.
    c.   much higher for blacks than for whites.
    d.   much higher for whites than for blacks.

17. _____   The text observes that, according to _____ law, a husband had the right to physically chastise an errant wife.
    a.   conjugal
    b.   English common
    c.   twentieth-century
    d.   post-Victorian

18. _____   If couple violence is _____, both men and women engage in intimate partner violence and at similar rates.
    a.   symmetrical
    b.   asymmetrical
    c.   conjugal
    d.   egalitarian

19. _____   _____ involves a parent's often being overly harsh and critical, failing to provide guidance, or being uninterested in a child's needs.
    a.   Sexual abuse
    b.   Child abuse
    c.   Emotional child abuse or neglect
    d.   Incest

20. _____   Those who favor the _____ approach believe that one or both parents should be held legally responsible for abusing a child.
    a.   therapeutic
    b.   counseling
    c.   litigious
    d.   punitive

21. _____   Which of the following are the most frequent perpetrators of child-to-parent abuse?
    a.   male children
    b.   female children
    c.   male adolescents
    d.   female adolescents

22. _____ When the rewards and privileges of the relationship are proportional to the contributions of the partners, there is _____ in the relationship.
   a. fairness
   b. equity
   c. harmony
   d. balance

23. _____ John is the head of the household and the authority figure in his marriage, responsible for all decision making. The marriage operates on the _____.
   a. egalitarian norm of marital power
   b. matriarchal norm of marital power
   c. patriarchal norm of marital power
   d. balanced norm of marital power

24. _____ The neotraditional family is best described as one
   a. which is totally egalitarian.
   b. which is female dominated.
   c. in which there is mutual decision making.
   d. in which there is formal male dominance with an egalitarian spirit.

25. _____ Battered womens' fear is justified by the fact that _____ percent of murders of women by their partners occur when the woman attempts to leave.
   a. 55
   b. 65
   c. 75
   d. 85

26. _____ Abuse that is almost entirely male and oriented toward controlling the partner through fear and intimidation is
   a. patriarchal terrorism.
   b. common violence.
   c. emotional abuse.
   d. psychological abuse.

27. _____ Same-sex couple violence occurs
   a. less frequently than in heterosexual relationships.
   b. at the same rate as in heterosexual relationships.
   c. more frequently than in heterosexual relationships.
   d. does not occur in same sex couples.

28. _____ The most pervasive form of family violence is
   a. spousal violence.
   b. sibling violence.
   c. child abuse.
   d. elder abuse.

29. _____ Which approach to combating child abuse leaves the child in the family and provides support within the home?
   a.   criminal justice approach
   b.   therapeutic approach
   c.   family preservation approach
   d.   social welfare approach

30. _____ The _____ approach to child abuse is punitive and believes that the parents should be held legally responsible.
   a.   criminal justice approach
   b.   therapeutic approach
   c.   social welfare approach
   d.   family preservation approach

TRUE-FALSE

1. _____ When partners perceive themselves as reciprocally respected, listened to, and supported by the other, they are more apt to define themselves as equal partners.

2. _____ In their investigations, Robert Blood and Donald Wolfe reported extensively on black families.

3. _____ The text points out that wage-earning wives have more to say than their husbands in important decisions and in the division of household labor.

4. _____ Unlike their married counterparts, cohabiting partners are less likely to break up if the woman earns more than the man than if the earnings are similar or the male earns more.

5. _____ The majority of Americans, regardless of class, do not see power inequities in their own marriages, although they obviously exist.

6. _____ The relative love and need theory predicts whether husbands or wives will generally be more powerful.

7. _____ The text points out that, looking to the future, American society could come to legitimate norms of equality in marriage as strongly as it endorsed patriarchal authority in the past.

8. _____ According to the text, peer marriages came from feminist ideology.

9. _____ The text observes that both equal and unequal partners may engage in a cycle of devitalizing power politics.

10. _____ Some marriages and relationships are entirely free of power politics.

11. _____ The National Family Violence Surveys show that unemployed people and high school dropouts are more likely to be violent with their intimate partners.

12. _____ *Numbers and rates* (rates refer to murders per 100,000) of homicide victimization remain much higher for blacks than for whites.

13. _____ In terms of relative status, a woman's risk of experiencing severe violence is greatest when her husband is employed and she is unemployed.

14. _____ The latest reports have confirmed that intimate-partner violence is *asymmetrical*, rather than *symmetrical*.

15. _____ It now appears that arrest will deter future domestic violence only on the part of men who are employed and married – men with a "stake in conformity."

16. _____ Perceptions of what constitutes child abuse or neglect have remained very consistent throughout history and in various cultures.

17. _____ The most common forms of maltreatment by female parents were "neglect" and "medical neglect."

18. _____ According to the federal report *Child Maltreatment, 2005*, "sexual abuse" was almost entirely perpetrated by male parents or male relatives.

19. _____ Research reveals that parents who abuse their children were often abused and neglected themselves as children.

SHORT ANSWER

1. Distinguish between personal power, social power, and conjugal power. Give an example of each.

2. Briefly explain Blood and Wolfe's *resource hypothesis*. Give an example.

3.   What is a *no-power* relationship? Give an example.

4.   Summarize the three-phase cycle of violence.

5.   Compare and contrast the criminal justice and therapeutic approaches to child abuse.

ESSAY

1.   The text suggests six bases, or sources, of power. List all six and give an example of each.

2.   Discuss the classical perspectives on marital power.

3.   What is *peer marriage*? How does the concept of "power politics" fit in here?

4.   What are the major sources of data on family violence?

5.   What are the primary risk factors for child abuse and for elder abuse?

ANSWERS TO SAMPLE QUESTIONS

Completion (using key terms)

1.	Marital	6.	Child abuse
2.	Reward	7.	Child neglect
3.	Referent	8.	Sexual abuse
4.	egalitarian	9.	Sibling
5.	relative love and need	10.	domestic violence

Multiple Choice (page references in parentheses)

1.	c (352)	16.	c (369)
2.	a (352)	17.	b (372)
3.	d (353)	18.	a (374)
4.	b (353)	19.	c (380)
5.	a (353)	20.	d (383)
6.	d (353)	21.	c (384)
7.	c (354)	22.	b (352
8.	b (355)	23.	c (356)
9.	c (354)	24.	d (361)
10.	d (356)	25.	d (371)
11.	a (356)	26.	a (376)
12.	b (362)	27.	b (377)
13.	b (363)	28.	b (380)
14.	a (367)	29.	c (383)
15.	d (369)	30.	a (383)

True-False (page references in parentheses)

1.	T (352)	11.	T (367)
2.	F (354)	12.	F (369)
3.	T (354)	13.	F (371)
4.	F (356)	14.	F (374)
5.	T (356)	15.	T (378)
6.	F (356)	16.	F (379)
7.	T (357)	17.	T (382)
8.	F (362)	18.	T (381)
9.	T (363)	19.	T (380)
10.	F (363)		

CHAPTER 15

FAMILY STRESS, CRISIS, AND RESILIENCE

CHAPTER SUMMARY

Family stress is a state of tension that arises when demands tax a family's resources. When adjustments are not easy to come by, family stress can lead to a **family crisis**.

The theoretical perspectives that are typically used when examining family stress and crises are structure functionalism, family development or family life course, family ecology, interactionism, and family systems.

Stressors are precipitating events that create stress. There are a number of different types of stressors: addition of a family member, loss of a family member, ambiguous loss, sudden change, conflict over family roles, caring for a disabled or dependent family member, demoralizing events, and daily family hassles. Stressor overload often creeps up on people without their realizing it.

Families that are having difficulties or functioning less than effectively before the onset of additional stressors or demands are said to be **vulnerable**; families capable of doing well in the face of adversity are called **resilient**. A family crisis ordinarily follows three distinct phases: the event that causes the crisis, the period of disorganization that follows, and the reorganizing or recovery phase after the family reaches a low point. Family members gradually begin to assimilate the reality of a crisis and to appraise the situation. Then, the **period of disorganization** sets in. Once the crisis hits bottom, recovery can begin.

There are different theories of family crisis and adaptation: the **ABC-X model** and the double ABC-X model. After **pile-up** occurs and family members begin to assimilate the reality of a crisis, appraisal begins. A family's crisis-meeting capabilities – resources and coping behaviors – constitute its ability to prevent a stressor from creating severe disharmony or disruption. A family's crisis-meeting resources can be categorized into three types: personal/individual, family, and community.

Meeting family crises creatively depends on a number of factors: a positive outlook; spiritual values and support groups; open, supportive communication; adaptability; informal social support; an extended family; and community resources.

A family crisis is a turning point in the course of family living that requires members to change how they have been thinking and acting.

LEARNING OBJECTIVES

Based on your careful and thorough reading of Chapter 15, you should:

1.   understand the relationship between family stress and family crisis.

2.   be familiar with the theoretical perspectives on family stress and crises.

3.   know the different types of stressors.

4. understand how family transitions can create stress and how this situation can lead to stressor overload.

5. be familiar with the course of a family crisis, including the period of disorganization and recovery.

6. understand the different theories of family crisis and adaptation.

7. be familiar with the factors associated with meeting crises creatively.

8. understand how crisis can be an opportunity rather than a disaster.

KEY TERMS (page references in parentheses)

ABC-X model (400)
boundary ambiguity (393)
family crisis (390)
family stress (390)
family transitions (390)
fictive kin (406)

nadir of family disorganization (399)
period of family disorganization (398)
pile-up (stressor overload) (397)
resilient families (398)
stressors (392)
vulnerable families (398)

COMPLETION (using key terms)

1. _____ is a state of tension that arises when demands tax a family's resources.

2. When adjustments are not easy to come by, family stress can lead to a _____.

3. A _____ is a precipitating event that creates stress.

4. From the family systems perspective, ambiguous loss is uniquely difficult to deal with because it creates _____ in a family.

5. _____ are expected or predictable changes in the course of family life.

6. After family members begin to assimilate the reality of a crisis and then to appraise the situation, the period of _____ sets in.

7. At the _____, or low point, of family disorganization, conflicts may develop over how the situation should be handled.

8. Reuben Hill formulated the _____ model of family crisis.

9. _____ includes not just the stressor but also previously existing family strains and future hardships induced by the stressor event.

10. _____ families cope well with stress and emphasize mutual acceptance, respect, and shared values.

KEY THEORETICAL PERSPECTIVES

structure-functional perspective
family development perspective
family ecology perspective
interactionist perspective
family systems perspective
ABC-X model
resiliency model of family stress, adjustment, and adaptation

INTERNET AND INFOTRAC EXERCISES

<u>Internet Exercises</u>

1.   Go to http://stress.about.com/od/lifestagefamilystress/. There, you will find a list of life's most stressful events. After you have scrolled down the list, check to see how stressful your life is.
    •   Based on the contents of the website you have just examined, what is your stress score? How stressful is your life?

2.   Go to http://www.uky.edu/Agriculture/Sociology/holstres.htm. There, you will find a short article entitled "Holidays Can Be a Source of Family Stress." After reading the article, respond to the following questions:
    •   Make a list of the ways in which holidays can be a source of family stress.
    •   Write a short paper describing your personal impressions of holiday stress within your own family environment.

3.   *Al-Anon* is an organization allied with *Alcoholics Anonymous*, and devoted to helping *family members* who are related to alcoholics and people with alcohol problems. Another related organization is *Alateen*, which is composed of teenage relatives of alcohol abuse sufferers. In order to glimpse *Al-Anon* as an organization, go to http://www.al-anon.org/english.html. After you have familiarized yourself with the contents, respond to the following questions:
    •   Do you think that *Al-Anon/Alateen* can be helpful to family members who are related to alcoholics? Why or why not?
    •   If possible, try to relate what you've learned from examining this site to a real-life situation involving a member of your own family or the family of someone you know.

4.   Go to the website of the International Society for Traumatic Stress Studies, http://www.istss.org/. Click on the heading for Mass Disasters, Trauma and Loss. Read about what your chances are for experiencing such trauma and what you can do to reduce the stress from such traumatic events.

<u>InfoTrac Exercises</u>

1. Use the key words *The American Family Crisis*. A 1995 article by sociologist David Popenoe will appear. After you have read this article, respond to the following questions:
    - Do you think that contemporary families face more crises than, say, the average family in preindustrial America? Why or why not?
    - Does the *future* of the American family concern you? Why or why not?

2. Use the key words *The Road Less Traveled: A New Psychology of Love, Traditional Values, and Spiritual Growth*. Read the article by John W. Donohue. Link your assessment of this article to the text's discussion of *spiritual values and support groups*. Then, respond to these questions:
    - The text cites spiritual values as an important element in meeting family crises creatively. What are your thoughts on the place of spiritual values in dealing with family crises?
    - Do you think it is important for family members to have *faith* in a higher power as they deal with family crises? Why or why not?

3. Use the key words *parents in prison*. After you have browsed through several of the articles available, respond to the following questions:
    - The *Issues for Thought* insert in this chapter is entitled "When a Parent Is In Prison." Read the contents of this insert and compare its insight with the articles that you selected.
    - What do you think it would be like (or what it *is* like, if you have had the experience) to have a parent in prison? Try to imagine the impact of this situation on the different members of your family.

TRUE-FALSE

1. _____ Families are more likely to be happy when they work toward mutually supportive relationships, and when they have the resources to do so.

2. _____ Adding a member to the family – through birth, adoption, marriage, remarriage, or the onset of cohabitation – is a stressor.

3. _____ Characteristically, stressor overload creeps up on people without their realizing it.

4. _____ In the period of disorganization following a family crisis, family functioning increases from its initial level.

5. _____ Pile-up renders a family more vulnerable to emerging from a crisis at a lower level of effectiveness.

6. _____ Believing from the start that a family crisis is surmountable can make adjustment much more difficult.

7. _____ Rituals can be family resources.

8. _____ Some researchers have found that strong religious faith is related to high family cohesiveness.

9. _____ The text points out that prison visitation programs fail to normalize parent-child contact.

10. _____ When family members have options and choices, they have absolute control over their lives.

MULTIPLE CHOICE

1. _____ The text points out that a family member's injury or illness, or a death in the family, is a source of family
   a. stress.
   b. alienation.
   c. disgruntlement.
   d. panic.

2. _____ According to the text, we can think of family _____ as a sharper jolt to a family than more ordinary family stress.
   a. instability
   b. breakdown
   c. crisis
   d. alienation

3. _____ Conflict between work and family roles that is largely created by workplace demands is an example of how environmental factors can cause family stress. This observation is reflective of which theoretical perspective?
   a. family systems
   b. family ecology
   c. interactionist
   d. conflict

4. _____ Which of the following is NOT one of the types of stressors examined in the text?
   a. daily family hassles
   b. demoralizing events
   c. conflict over family roles
   d. gradual change

5. _____ Jeffrey's father was an investment banker in New York City and is presumed dead, since he was conducting business in the World Trade Center on September 11, 2001. Jeffrey finds this situation difficult to deal with, in large part because his father's body has not been recovered and Jeffrey cannot be sure whether his father is "in or out of the family." These circumstances best illustrate which of the following concepts?
   a. boundary ambiguity
   b. sudden change
   c. ongoing conflict
   d. demoralizing events

6. _____ Which of the following is NOT one of the "daily family hassles" mentioned in the text?
   a. feeling overworked at home
   b. not having enough money to pay bills
   c. stressful work situation
   d. a child being charged with illegal drug use

7. _____ During _____, family organization slumps, habitual roles and routines become nebulous and confused, and members carry out their responsibilities with less enthusiasm.
   a. boundary ambiguity
   b. family transitions
   c. the period of disorganization
   d. pile-up

8. _____ At the _____ of family disorganization, conflicts may develop over how the situation should be handled.
   a. recovery stage
   b. nadir
   c. decision point
   d. crisis point

9. _____ In the ABC-X model of family crisis, the "B" represents
   a. the family's ability to cope with a crisis, their crisis-meeting resources.
   b. the family's appraisal of the stressor event.
   c. the stressor event.
   d. the crisis.

10. _____ In the ABC-X model of family crisis, the "C" represents
    a. the stressor event.
    b. the crisis.
    c. the family's ability to cope with a crisis, their crisis meeting resources.
    d. the family's appraisal of the stressor event.

11. _____ Which of the following is NOT one of the suggestions offered in the text for lessening family stress while at homeless shelters?
    a. allowing parents as much control as possible over bedtimes and eating arrangements
    b. provide more welfare benefits
    c. offspring day care
    d. keeping shelters open to families during the day

12. _____ The text categorizes a family's crisis-meeting resources into three types. Which of the following is NOT one of these?
    a. ritual
    b. personal/individual
    c. family
    d. community

13. _____ _____ families are more prone to negative outcomes from crisis-provoking events than are resilient families.
    a. Stressed
    b. Crisis-oriented
    c. Vulnerable
    d. Maladapted

14. _____ According to the text, _____ families are better able to respond effectively to crises.
- a. vulnerable
- b. crisis-oriented
- c. adaptable
- d. extended

15. _____ In 1995, the U.S. government mandated parent education programs for federal prison inmates. This is an example of
- a. informal social support.
- b. community resources.
- c. spiritual values and support groups.
- d. open, supportive communication.

16. _____ Which theoretical perspective looks at the family as a system where each part influences all of the other parts?
- a. family ecology
- b. functionalist
- c. family systems
- d. conflict

17. _____ Ambiguous family losses include all of the following EXCEPT
- a. having a family member who has been called to war.
- b. having an alcoholic family member who is psychologically absent.
- c. having a family member with Alzheimers.
- d. having a loss of a child through a miscarriage.

18. _____ According to Figure 15.2, which of the following is NOT considered a catastrophe and unexpected stressful situation?
- a. incarceration
- b. military deployment
- c. desertion
- d. chronic mental illness

19. _____ In the stressful situation of providing health care for a family member, what is the most unsettling aspect of those responsibilities?
- a. lack of supervision or emergency backup
- b. following dietary guidelines
- c. allowing pets on the bed
- d. deciding if wearing gloves is necessary

20. _____ A more descriptive term for stressor overload is
- a. stressor wreck.
- b. stressor disaster.
- c. stressor pile-up.
- d. stressor maximization.

21. _____ Families that are doing well in the face of adversity are
   a. stable
   b. impenetrable
   c. vulnerable
   d. resilient

22. _____ Once the family has reached the low point of family disorganization, which of the
   following is most often the outcome?
   a. maintenance of the disorganization
   b. recovery
   c. crisis
   d. resilient

23. _____ Which sociologist first proposed the ABC-X family crisis model?
   a. Robert Sterberg
   b. Joan Patterson
   c. Charles Horton Cooley
   d. Reuben Hill

24. _____ The double ABC-X model describes which of the following types of crises?
   a. pile-up
   b. maximized stress
   c. family adjustment
   d. family disaster

25. _____ All of the following are characteristics of resilient families EXCEPT
   a. shared values.
   b. mutual acceptance.
   c. diminished respect.
   d. commitment.

SHORT ANSWER

1. Identify and briefly discuss four of the types of stressors discussed in the text.

2. What is *stressor overload*? Give an example.

3.   What is *pile-up*? Give an example.

4.   What is *the period of disorganization*?

5.   Describe the *recovery* period in the course of a family crisis.

Chapter 15

ESSAY

1.	Identify and discuss three of the theoretical perspectives that are mentioned in the text, as they are applied to family stress and crises.

2.	Trace the stages of a family crisis.

3.	Discuss the ABC-X model of family crisis and adaptation.

4.	What are the major crisis-meeting resources?

5.	What are the steps in meeting crises creatively?

ANSWERS TO SAMPLE QUESTIONS

Completion (using key terms)

1.	Family stress	6.	disorganization
2.	family crisis	7.	nadir
3.	stressor	8.	ABC-X
4.	boundary ambiguity	9.	Pile-up
5.	Family transitions	10.	Resilient

Multiple Choice (page references in parentheses)

1.	a (390)	9.	a (400)
2.	c (390)	10.	d (400)
3.	b (391)	11.	b (400-401)
4.	d (392)	12.	a (403)
5.	a (393)	13.	c (404)
6.	d (395)	14.	c (405)
7.	c (398)	15.	b (408-409)
8.	b (399)		

True-False (page references in parentheses)

1.	T (390)	6.	F (402)
2.	T (392)	7.	T (403)
3.	T (397)	8.	T (405)
4.	F (398)	9.	F (408-409)
5.	T (400)	10.	F (408)

CHAPTER 16

DIVORCE: BEFORE AND AFTER

CHAPTER SUMMARY

Between 40 percent and 50 percent of recent first marriages are likely to end in divorce. The frequency of divorce increased sharply throughout most of the twentieth century. This chapter begins with an exploration of how divorce rates are reported and an examination of the country's current divorce rate. Then, the question of why more couples are divorcing is addressed: decreased economic interdependence (the relationship between divorce and income; wives in the labor force), decreased social, legal, and moral constraints, high expectations for marriage, the changed nature of marriage itself, as well as other factors associated with divorce, the **intergenerational transmission of divorce**, and some common marital complaints. Various alternatives to divorce are reviewed, as well as an assessment of whether divorce is a temporary crisis or a permanent stress. The different "stages" of divorce are examined: the **economic divorce**, the **emotional divorce**, the **legal divorce**, the **community divorce**, and the **psychic divorce**. The economic consequences of divorce include differences for husbands and for wives, various attitudes about alimony, and child support. The chapter reviews the effects of divorce on children, as well as "her divorce" and "his divorce." The consequences of divorce for the next generation are addressed. The question of whether divorce should be "harder to get" is evaluated, followed by a discussion of surviving divorce.

Divorce rates have risen sharply in this century, and divorce rates in the United States are now the highest in the world. In the past decade, however, they have begun to level off. The reasons why more people are divorcing than in the past have to do with changes in society: economic interdependence and legal, moral, and social constraints are lessening, expectations for intimacy are increasing, and expectations for permanence are declining. People's personal decisions to divorce, or to **redivorce**, involve weighing marital complaints against the possible consequences of divorce. Two consequences that receive a great deal of consideration are how the divorce will affect children, if there are any, and whether it will cause serious financial difficulties.

The divorce experience is almost always far more painful than people expect. Bohannan has identified six ways in which divorce affects people. The six stations of divorce are the emotional divorce, the legal divorce, the community divorce, the psychic divorce, and the economic divorce.

The economic divorce is typically more disastrous for women than for men, and this is especially so for custodial mothers. Over the past fifteen years, child support policies have undergone sweeping changes which are only now beginning to result in evaluation research.

Researchers have proposed five possible theories to explain negative effects of divorce on children. These include the **life stress perspective**, the **parental loss perspective**, the **parental adjustment perspective**, the **economic hardship perspective**, and the **interparental conflict perspective**.

Husbands' and wives' divorce experiences, like husbands' and wives' marriages, are different. Both the overload that characterizes the wife's divorce and the loneliness that often accompanies the husband's divorce, especially when there are children, can be lessened in the future by more androgynous settlement. Divorce counseling can help make the experience less painful. **Divorce mediation** is another alternative. **Joint custody** offers the opportunity of greater involvement by both parents, although its impact is still being evaluated, along with the effect of parents' divorce on children's marital prospects. Research findings vary in reference to whether divorce is necessarily "bad" for children. Of course, there are consequences of divorce for children, but the "good" divorce is one in which the partners avoid using the children as pawns in the process.

LEARNING OBJECTIVES

Based on your careful and thorough reading of Chapter 16, you should:

1. be familiar with how divorce rates are reported and be aware of the current divorce rate in the United States.

2. understand the reasons why couples are divorcing.

3. be acquainted with the alternatives to divorce.

4. understand the different "stations" of divorce.

5. be familiar with the economic consequences of divorce.

6. understand the various stresses for children of divorce and various custody issues.

7. be able to distinguish between "his" and "her" divorce.

8. be familiar with the circumstances surrounding adult children of divorced parents and intergenerational relationships.

9. be able to respond to the question of whether divorce should be harder to get.

10. be familiar with what can be done to address the negative consequences of divorce for children and what the text calls the "good divorce."

KEY TERMS (page references in parentheses)

binuclear family (513)
child snatching (503)
child support (492)
children's allowance (493)
community divorce (486)
covenant marriage (511)
crude divorce rate (475)
custodial parent (491)
custody (501)
displaced homemaker (491)
divorce-extended family (515)
divorce mediation (486)
economic divorce (490)
economic hardship perspective (499)
emotional divorce (485)
guaranteed child support (493)
income effect (477)
independence effect (477)
intergenerational transmission
  of divorce (481)

interparental conflict perspective
  [on children's adjustment to
  divorce] (499)
joint custody (504)
legal divorce (485)
life stress perspective
  [on children's adjustment to
  divorce] (499)
no-fault divorce (485)
parental adjustment perspective
  [on children's adjustment to
  divorce] (499)
parental loss perspective
  [on children's adjustment to
  divorce] (499)
psychic divorce (488)
redivorce (476)
refined divorce rate (475)
relatives of divorce (487)
spousal support (491)
supervised visitation (503)

COMPLETION (using key terms)

1.   The _____ divorce rate refers to the number of divorces per 1,000 married women over age 15.

2.   The _____ effect refers to a situation where employment contributes to the divorce of an unhappily married women by offering her the economic power and the self-confidence to help her decide on marital dissolution.

3.   A _____ divorce is the dissolution of marriage by the state through a court order terminating the marriage.

4.   _____ is an alternative, non-adversarial means of dispute resolution by which a couple, with the assistance of a third party, negotiate the terms of the divorce settlement.

5.   The _____ divorce refers to ruptures of relationships and changes in social networks that come about as a result of divorce.

6.   _____ divorce refers to the regaining of psychological autonomy through emotional separation from the personality and influence of the former spouse.

7.   Upon divorce, a couple undergoes a(n) _____ divorce in which they become independent parties with regard to property, income, control of expenditures, responsibility for taxes, debts, and so forth.

8.   A _____ family consists of two households and one family.

9.   _____ involves money paid by a non-custodial to a custodial parent to support the children of a separated marital, cohabiting, or sexual relationship.

10.   _____ visitation between a non-custodial parent and his or her children takes place only in the presence of a third party, such as a social worker or a court employee.

11.   _____ refers to kidnapping one's own children from the other parent.

12.   In Louisiana, Arizona, and Arkansas, _____ marriage can be selected at the time of marriage or later as an alternative to standard marriage.

KEY THEORETICAL PERSPECTIVES

exchange theory
functional theory
conflict theory
Amato's theoretical perspectives concerning effects of divorce on children
      life stress
      parental loss
      parental adjustment
      economic hardship
      interparental conflict

INTERNET AND INFOTRAC EXERCISES

Internet Exercises

1.   The text discusses how divorce rates are reported. Go to:
http://www.divorcemag.com/statistics/statsUS.shtml. There, you will find a variety of
statistics in reference to the divorce rate in the United States. Examine these data and then
respond to the following:
- Choose ten statistical statements relating to divorce and propose an explanation for the
trend reported.

2.   As of this writing, *covenant marriage* is a legal option in the states of Louisiana, Arizona, and
Arkansas. A number of other states have introduced legislation that would approve a variation on
this option. For a detailed look at the provisions of covenant marriage, go to:
http://www.divorcereform.org/cov.html. After you have explored this website, respond to the
following questions:
- Do you feel that the covenant marriage option will help to curb the divorce rate? Why or
why not?
- If you are already married, would you have considered the covenant marriage option? If
you are planning on marriage in the future, would you consider this alternative? Why or
why not?
- Do you think that holding people "at fault" for divorce is a rational plan? Why or why
not?

3.   There are a variety of websites that deal with *adult children of divorced parents*. For a glimpse at
one adult child's "story," go to: http://www.acod.net/. After you have taken a look at the main
page, click on **My Story**. After you have read the contents, respond to the following questions:
- If you are an adult child of divorced parents, do you see any similarities between your
situation and the person who created and manages this website? If your parents are still
living and still married, what do you think your reactions would be if they decided to
divorce?
- Do you think that the experiences of adult children of divorced parents are similar, or is
every situation different? Does the experience depend upon how the parents approach the
dissolution of their marriage? If you think so, what can parents do to minimize the
negative impact of divorce on their children?

4.   The text discusses some of the challenges that confront divorcing spouses who have dependent children and who will become *co-parents*. In order to examine a proposed agreement for people who will become co-parents, go to: http://www.acbr.com/paragree.htm.

5.   Visitation issues exist not only for parents after a divorce but also for grandparents. At http://www.grandparenting.org/Grandparent%20Visitation.htm learn more about grandparents visitation rights.
    - Do you feel that it is important for the grandparents of children of divorce to be able to have visitation rights?
    - Scroll to the bottom of the page and read the criteria for grandparent visitation in general. The find your state in the list and see what criteria are applied in your state.
    - What do you think are the *most important* features of any co-parenting agreement?
    - If you are a co-parent, would you say that you are living up to the terms of the proposed agreement? How about your ex-spouse? If you have no experience with co-parenting, suppose that you become a co-parent. What do you think of the proposed agreement? Is there anything you would add to these provisions?

InfoTrac Exercises

1.   Use the key words *tough child support laws put poor fathers in a bind*. Read the article from the *New York Times*. Then respond to the following questions:
    - What are the implications for child support laws for socioeconomically disadvantaged fathers?
    - Do you think that the tough child support laws described in this article are beneficial for society or a liability? Why?

2.   Use the key words *divorce mediation*. From the sources available, focus on those articles that directly address divorce mediation as an alternative to traditional, adversarial divorce. After you have examined some of these sources, respond to the following questions:
    - What is your overall reaction to divorce mediation? Do you think it is a preferable alternative to traditional, adversary divorce? Why or why not?
    - If you are previously married, and assuming that you did not utilize divorce mediation in dissolving your marriage, do you think that you would have benefited from this alternative? If so, how? If you have had no personal experience with divorce, imagine that you are going through the process. Do you feel that divorce mediation would be an attractive procedure in comparison with traditional divorce? Why or why not?
    - A number of observers have commented that divorce mediation helps to avoid some of the negative impact that divorce has on dependent children. Do you agree with this assessment? Why or why not?

3.   Use the key words *children and divorce*. Focus on articles that specifically address the impact of divorce on children. After you have examined a number of articles that focus on this topic, respond to the following questions:
    - Do you agree with the assertion that divorce is *not* that harmful to involved children? Why or why not?
    - Do you think that the harmful effects of divorce on children have been "overplayed?" Why or why not?
    - How do you think divorcing parents can try to avoid the negative impact of divorce on their dependent children?

MULTIPLE CHOICE

1. _____ A survey cited in the text determined that the divorce rate _____ from 1980 to 2005.
    a. declined
    b. showed no change
    c. increased slightly
    d. increased dramatically

2. _____ The number of divorces per 1,000 married women over age 15 reflects the _____ divorce rate.
    a. crude
    b. total
    c. refined
    d. gender-specific

3. _____ If we consider age at marriage, it is marrying _____ that carries the highest risk of divorce.
    a. before age twenty
    b. between age eighteen and twenty-five
    c. between age twenty and thirty
    d. over age fifty

4. _____ In 2000, _____ percent of children lived with two married parents (biological parents or stepparents).
    a. 29
    b. 39
    c. 49
    d. 69

5. _____ The text points to a consequence of remarriages, which have higher failure rates than first marriages. This consequence is an emerging trend of
    a. singlehood.
    b. redivorce.
    c. cohabitation.
    d. commuter marriage.

6. _____ The text points out that defining marriage as semipermanent
    a. will lead inevitably to the demise of marriage as an institution.
    b. will cause the divorce rate to rise higher and higher.
    c. can become a self-fulfilling prophecy.
    d. encourages cohabitation.

7. _____ One model discussed in the text argues that spouses weigh their marital happiness against alternatives to the marriage as well as barriers to divorce. This design is derived from which theoretical perspective?
    a. functionalist
    b. exchange
    c. conflict
    d. interactionist

8. _____ The introduction of _____ was intended to reduce the hostility of divorcing partners, as well as to permit an individual to end a failed marriage readily.
   a. no-fault divorce
   b. divorce mediation
   c. covenant marriage
   d. legal divorce

9. _____ All fifty states now have grandparent visitation laws, but in the Supreme Court decision of *Troxel v. Granville* (2000), the grandparent visitation statute in the state of _____ was struck down.
   a. California
   b. New York
   c. Louisiana
   d. Washington

10. _____ A non-adversarial means of dispute resolution where couples negotiate settlements of custody, support, property and visitation issues is
    a. divorce resolution.
    b. divorce mediation.
    c. divorce negotiation.
    d. no-fault divorce.

11. _____ _____ percent of all children who reside in mother-only, single-parent families live in poverty.
    a. Three
    b. Thirteen
    c. Twenty-three
    d. Thirty-three

12. _____ According to the text, _____ states now have laws promising a divorced wife either an equitable or an equal share of the marital property.
    a. a majority of
    b. a minority of
    c. fewer than 20
    d. fewer than 10

13. _____ The chief reason for divorced men's declining standard of living is
    a. men's emotional dependence on being married.
    b. the loss of the partner's income.
    c. rejection by the community.
    d. a drop in men's self-confidence.

14. _____ The text points out that policy and procedural changes in child support were prompted by a number of separate but overlapping concerns. Which of the following is NOT one of these?
    a. the move to privatize support obligations for children in an effort to lessen welfare spending
    b. concern about the growing proportion of children in female-headed, single-parent households
    c. reduction of father's economic responsibility in paying child support
    d. alarm about the growing proportion of children living in poverty

15. _____ Judy is a single-parent and has sole custody of her three children. She receives a government grant based on her parenthood of these three youngsters. This grant is referred to as
   a. guaranteed child support.
   b. a children's allowance.
   c. aid to dependent children.
   d. social welfare.

16. _____ Wallerstein and Kelly's research suggests that in the initial aftermath of divorce, children appear worst in terms of their psychological adjustment
   a. at one year after separation.
   b. by two years postdivorce.
   c. at five years postdivorce.
   d. at ten years postdivorce.

17. _____ Reviewing research done in the 1990s, Amato found that children of divorce continue to be lower than children from intact families in certain areas. Which of the following is NOT one of these areas?
   a. academic success
   b. psychological adjustment
   c. social competence
   d. socioeconomic status

18. _____ Which of the following is NOT one of the theoretical perspectives identified by Amato concerning the reasons for negative outcomes among children of divorced parents?
   a. life stress
   b. parental loss
   c. economic affluence
   d. interparental conflict

19. _____ Experts agree that adjusting to divorce is easier for children and parents when former spouses
   a. recognize the inevitability of conflict.
   b. cooperate.
   c. are business partners.
   d. are affiliated with some organized religion.

20. _____ In _____ custody, both parents have the right to participate in important decisions and retain a symbolically important legal authority.
   a. joint legal
   b. physical
   c. joint legal and physical
   d. sole

21. _____ Which of the following is NOT one of Constance Ahrons' types of postdivorce relationships?
   a. perfect pals
   b. cooperative colleagues
   c. good divorcees
   d. fiery foes

22. _____ The effect in which women have increased economic power which in turn may contribute to divorce is
    a.   income effect.
    b.   economic effect.
    c.   independence effect.
    d.   power effect.

23. _____ Results of the Marital Instability Over the Life Course surveys which of the following was not associated with a lower likelihood of divorce?
    a.   the wife's income was a smaller percentage of the family income
    b.   church attendance was high
    c.   friendship networks increased
    d.   there was a new child

24. _____ When both parents continue to take equal responsibility for important decisions regarding the child's general upbringing is
    a.   sole custody.
    b.   joint custody.
    c.   physical custody.
    d.   shared custody.

25. _____ Which of the following is not required by a covenant marriage?
    a.   couples are required to prove fault
    b.   live apart for a substantial length of time
    c.   a two month waiting period before getting married
    d.   premarital counseling directed toward saving the marriage

26. _____ According to research by Betsey Stevenson and Justin Wolfers, no-fault divorce is associated with
    a.   improved economic condition for women.
    b.   an increase in intimate partner homicide.
    c.   increase in overall domestic violence for men and women.
    d.   a decrease in suicide rates for women.

27. _____ According to a study sponsored by the Justice Department, over _____ children were abducted by family members in 1999.
    a.   100,000
    b.   200,000
    c.   300,000
    d.   400,000

28. _____ Which of the following perspectives on the negative effects of divorce on children deals with the parents' role and quality of parenting?
    a.   parental loss perspective
    b.   life stress perspective
    c.   economic hardship perspective
    d.   parental adjustment perspective

29. _____ Spousal support or maintenance is sometimes referred to as
   a. spouse maintenance
   b. rehabilitative alimony
   c. parental support
   d. income-to-needs support

30. _____ Which of these countries provide guaranteed child support through the government?
   a. France
   b. England
   c. Germany
   d. Spain

TRUE-FALSE

1. _____ The frequency of divorce has slowly declined throughout most of the twentieth century.

2. _____ Since the 1970s, divorce rates are higher than they have ever been in American society.

3. _____ As long as marriage continues to offer practical benefits, economic interdependence will help hold marriages together.

4. _____ Having parents who divorced does not increase the likelihood of divorcing.

5. _____ Remaining child-free is associated with a higher likelihood of divorce.

6. _____ Separating from one's former community of friends and in-laws is part of the pain of divorce.

7. _____ Children in father-only families are more likely to be poor than children in mother-only families.

8. _____ Only men with 1950s-type marriages gain economically in divorce.

9. _____ Some research suggests that the principal reason for a noncustodial parent's failure to pay child support is unemployment or underemployment.

10. _____ There is widespread agreement among the experts regarding the effects of separation and divorce on children.

11. _____ The "sleeper effect" described by Wallerstein has been generally supported by other studies.

12. _____ Children of divorce feel less protected economically.

13. _____ Married partners usually draw children openly into spousal wars in the same way that ex-spouses do.

14. _____ Some states have acted to prohibit all custodial parents from moving.

15. _____ Generally, evidence suggests that adult children of divorced parents feel more obligation to remain in contact with them and are more likely to receive help from them and to provide help to them.

SHORT ANSWER

1.   Distinguish between the *crude divorce rate* and the *refined divorce rate.*

2.   Summarize the increases/decreases in the divorce rate since about 1920.

3.   Briefly summarize what research results tell us about *redivorce.*

4.   What is *divorce mediation?* Give a practical example.

5.   Who are the *relatives of divorce?* Explain and give two examples.

ESSAY

1.   More couples are divorcing, or in other ways terminating, their marriages. Explain why this is happening.

2.   Explain the different "stations" of divorce using Bohannan's typology.

3.   Based on the text's discussion, what is the difference between "his" and "her" divorce?

4.   Compare and contrast the *parental loss perspective* and the *parental adjustment perspective* regarding explanations of negative outcomes among children of divorced parents. Give examples.

5.   Based on the text's discussion, what are the effects of divorce for the children involved?

ANSWERS TO SAMPLE QUESTIONS

Completion (using key terms)

1. refined
2. independence
3. legal
4. Divorce mediation
5. community
6. Psychic

7. economic
8. binuclear
9. Child support
10. Supervised
11. Child snatching
12. Covenant

Multiple Choice (page references in parentheses)

1. d (414)
2. c (414)
3. a (415)
4. d (416)
5. b (416)
6. c (417)
7. b (419)
8. a (417)
9. d (424)
10. b (423)
11. d (425)
12. a (426)
13. b (427)
14. c (427-428)
15. b (428)

16. a (429)
17. d (432)
18. c (432)
19. b (433)
20. a (438)
21. c (447)
22. c (416)
23. c (420)
24. b (438)
25. d (445)
26. d (438)
27. d (432)
29. b (427)
30. a (428)

True-False (page references in parentheses)

1. T (414)
2. F (414)
3. T (416)
4. F (418)
5. T (418)
6. T (424)
7. F (426)
8. T (428)
9. T (428)
10. F (428)
11. F (429)
12. T (429)
13. F (432)
14. T (439)
15. F (443)

CHAPTER 17

REMARRIAGES AND STEPFAMILIES

CHAPTER SUMMARY

Today, **remarriages** make up approximately half of all marriages. One in three Americans are now stepparents, stepchildren, stepsiblings, or living in a stepfamily. Many remarried people are happy with their relationships. There has been a slight decline in remarriage rates since 1975 because many divorced people who would have remarried in the past are now cohabiting and there are economic constraints and uncertainties of assuming financial responsibility for a new family. One result of the significant number of remarriages today is that more Americans are parenting other people's children.

Spouses are older at the time of remarriage than at first marriage. As a group, ex-wives, but not ex-husbands, are likely to gain financially by being remarried. Children lower the likelihood of remarriage for both men and women, but the impact of children is greater on women's probability of remarriage. Age is another factor that may work against women in several different ways. Homogamy has traditionally been a second important factor influencing marriage choices.

Marital happiness and marital satisfaction are synonymous phrases, but marital stability refers to the duration of the union. In general, research shows little difference in spouses' overall well-being or in marital happiness between first and later unions. Remarriages dissolve at higher rates than first marriages, especially for remarried couples with stepchildren. There are **single remarriages** and **double remarriages**. Remarital satisfaction is influenced by the wider society through the negative stereotyping of remarriages.

Our society offers members of **remarried families** no **cultural script** for relating to each other or for defining responsibilities and obligations. According to the **nuclear-family model monopoly**, the first-marriage family is the "real" model for family living, with all other family forms seen as deficient alternatives. There are three areas in which remarriage is a "normless norm": within the remarried families themselves, in relationships with kin, and in family law.

Generally speaking, research shows that there are minor differences between the well-being of stepchildren in comparison with children from first marriages. The vast majority of social scientists reject the idea that stepfamily formation should be discouraged.

Although they are developing, cultural norms do not clearly indicate how stepparents should play their role. Stepparenting is difficult: There are financial strains, role ambiguity, and negative feelings of the children, who often don't want the new family to work. The stepmother role has been described as the **stepmother trap**. The **hidden agenda** is one of the first difficulties a stepfather encounters. Research shows that having a mutual child is associated with increased happiness and marital stability.

Creating a supportive stepfamily is not automatic. One stepfamily scholar (Papernow, 1993) has suggested a **seven-stage model of stepfamily development** (fantasy, immersion, awareness, mobilization, action, contact, and resolution). It may help to think of a stepfamily as a **binuclear family**. At three years, remarried biological parents and their new partners had high rates of **co-parenting**.

Chapter 17

LEARNING OBJECTIVES

Based on your careful and thorough reading of Chapter 17, you should:

1.   be familiar with the basic facts surrounding remarriage.

2.   be familiar with the process of choosing partners, including remarriage advantages for women and men.

3.   be acquainted with homogamy in remarriage.

4.   understand the distinction between happiness/satisfaction in and stability of remarriages.

5.   understand why remarried families have been referred to as a "normless norm."

6.   be familiar with children's well-being in stepfamilies.

7.   be familiar with the reasons why stepparenting is difficult.

8.   understand the remarriage experience for stepmothers and for stepfathers.

9.   be familiar with the process of creating supportive stepfamilies

KEY TERMS (page references in parenthesis)

binuclear family (478)
co-parenting (448)
cultural script (465)
double remarriages (462)
extrusion (471)
hidden agenda (474)
incomplete institution (465)

nuclear-family model monopoly (465)
remarriages (456)
remarried families (456)
seven-stage model of stepfamily
  development (478)
single remarriages (462)
stepmother trap (473)

COMPLETION (using key terms)

1.   _____ are marriages in which at least one partner had previously been divorced or widowed.

2.   _____ remarriages are those in which both partners had been married before.

3.   _____ remarriages are those in which only one partner had been previously married.

4.   Our society offers members of remarried families no _____, or set of socially prescribed and understood guidelines, for relating to each other or for defining responsibilities and obligations.

5.   Because of the cultural ambiguity of remarried family relationships, social scientist Andrew Cherlin calls the remarried family a(n) _____.

6. According to the _____, the first-marriage family is the "real" model for family living, with all other family forms seen as deficient alternatives.

7. A(n) _____ family includes members of the two (or more) families that existed before a divorce and remarriage.

8. _____ refers to shared decision making and parental supervision in such areas as discipline and schoolwork or shared holidays and recreation.

9. Phyllis Raphael has written about the residential stepmother role as the stepmother _____.

10. The text points out that one of the first difficulties a stepfather encounters is the _____.

KEY THEORETICAL PERSPECTIVES

family ecology perspective
Papernow's seven-stage model of stepfamily development

INTERNET AND INFOTRAC EXERCISES

Internet Exercises

1. *Step Families Matter.com* advertises that it is the "original on-line community for blended family members." Visit their website at: http://www.step-family-matters.com. From the opening page, select one or more areas of this site to examine, depending upon your individual interests. After you have done this, respond to the following questions:
   - Do you think that "blended families" can be as functional as traditional families? Why or why not?
   - What personal experiences have you had with stepfamilies? Based upon these experiences, what is your overall orientation toward remarriage and stepfamily formation?

2. Go to: http://www.gettingremarried.com/. There, you will find a variety of resources concerning remarriage. Click on "blended family wedding." After you have read the contents of this section, respond to the following questions:
   - What are the primary differences between a "first wedding" and a "blended family wedding"?
   - Do you think how remarriage is handled can make a difference in terms of the future success of the relationship? If so, how?

3. Go to: http://www.secondwivesclub.com/. Click on a few of the articles that are referenced on the homepage that focus on remarriage and step-life. Then, respond to the following question:
   - What are the primary differences between biological parents' relationships with their children, versus stepparents' relationships with their stepchildren?

4. The Step Family Life at http://www.thestepfamilylife.com offers a wealth of articles about step families and how to assist families with the adjustments that are required to make remarriages work.

    - Go to the link for National Step Family Day and read about one stepmother's personal journey. What are the milestones that she relates in this article?
    - Choose other columns listed and read about some of the other challenges of step families? Can you relate to any of these? Can you think of other issues not mentioned here that are challenges for step families?

InfoTrac Exercises

1. Use the keyword *stepparenting*. From the list of articles available, select one or two and read the contents. Then, respond to the following questions:

    - Are the contents of the articles you read consistent with the discussion of stepparenting in the text? Did you learn anything new? If so, what?
    - Would you characterize the tone of these articles as "upbeat" regarding stepparenting? Make a list of the major points that are made in the selections you read.

2. Use the keyword *stepchildren*. From the list of articles available, focus on those that address the *children of stepfamilies*. After you have read two or three of the articles, respond to the following question:

    - One of the major headings in Chapter 17 is "Children's Well-Being in Stepfamilies." Based on this discussion, what did you learn from the articles that you read concerning this same issue?

3. Use the key word *remarriage*. From the list of articles available, focus on those that address the correlates of *success* in remarriage. Pick two or three articles and read their contents. Then, address the following:

    - Make a list of the major elements identified in the articles that are related to the success of remarriages. Do these observations align with what you learned from reading Chapter 17? Did you learn anything new from the articles? If so, what?

4. Use the key words *blended families*. From the list of articles available, select one or two that you find particularly interesting. You might want to focus on *financial concerns*, or possibly an article that deals with *co-parenting*. After reading the articles you selected, consider the following questions:

    - Do you think that "blended family" is an accurate description of *remarried family* situations? Why or why not?
    - Based upon what you learned from the articles you read, what are some of the major challenges that confront remarried families?

TRUE-FALSE

1. _____   Remarriages make up about 25 percent of all marriages.

2. _____   A majority of remarriages are third marriages.

3. _____   According to the text, it goes without saying that spouses are older at the time of remarriage than at first marriage.

4. _____   Courtship before remarriage is very similar to courtship before first marriage.

5. _____   Economists and other social scientists point out that, in general, ex-wives, but not ex-husbands, are likely to gain financially by being remarried.

6. _____   Remarriages are more homogamous than first marriages.

7. _____   Perhaps the most significant factor in the comparative instability of remarriages is the presence of stepchildren.

8. _____   The text points out that our language has not caught up with the proliferation of new family roles.

9. _____   Research suggests that remarried people may be reluctant to commit all of their economic resources to a second marriage and take care to protect their individual interests and those of their biological children.

10. _____   Therapists point out that stepparents and stepchildren should expect to feel the same as they would if they were biologically related.

MULTIPLE CHOICE

1. _____   Today, remarriages make up approximately _____ of all marriages.
   a.   one-eighth
   b.   one-fourth
   c.   one-third
   d.   one-half

2. _____   Which of the following statements concerning remarriage statistics is INCORRECT?
   a.   The remarriage rate dropped sharply during World War II.
   b.   The remarriage rate peaked as World War II ended.
   c.   During the 1950s, both the divorce rate and the remarriage rate declined.
   d.   The remarriage rate peaked again in about 1975, but declined slightly after that.

3. _____   The text reports that _____ percent of divorced women remarry within ten years.
   a.   25
   b.   65
   c.   50
   d.   75

4. _____   Donald and Rhea were married five years ago. Donald had been married before. They have one child of their own, whose name is Shelley. Danielle also lives with Donald and Rhea. She is Donald's biological daughter from his previous marriage. Rhea is Danielle's stepmother. Donald and Rhea's household would be categorized as
   a.   extended.
   b.   joint biological-step.
   c.   modified-extended.
   d.   conjugal.

5. _____   The average divorced person remarries within _____ years.
   a.   2
   b.   3
   c.   4
   d.   5

6. _____   Florence is a previously-divorced single woman who is 40-years-old. She would like to remarry, but feels that her age works against her in the remarriage market. According to the text's discussion, Florence's feelings illustrate
   a.   society's damaging stereotypes.
   b.   institutionalized discrimination.
   c.   the double standard of aging.
   d.   systematic prejudice.

7. _____   According to the text, recognizing that homogamy increases the likelihood of marital stability, we might hypothesize that divorced people tended more toward _____ than nondivorced people the first time around and that they repeat or accentuate this tendency when they remarry.
   a.   heterogamy
   b.   endogamy
   c.   exogamy
   d.   homogamy

8. _____   In which of the following racial/ethnic groups do women have the highest probability of remarrying?
   a.   Non-Hispanic whites
   b.   Asians
   c.   African Americans
   d.   Hispanic

9. _____   According to the text, *double remarriages involving stepchildren* display what level of risk for dissolution?
   a.   very low
   b.   low
   c.   elevated
   d.   very elevated

10. _____   According to the text, the statement "A stepfamily can never be as good as a family in which children live with both natural parents" is
   a.   a harmful myth.
   b.   partially supported by research.
   c.   completely supported by research.
   d.   impossible to document, one way or the other.

11. _____   According to the text, _____ families reflect a "normless norm."
   a.   conjugal
   b.   nuclear
   c.   remarried
   d.   extended

12. _____ Which of the following best characterizes the text's description of remarried families?
   a. relatively simple
   b. extremely complex
   c. homogeneous
   d. unchanging

13. _____ Which of the following is NOT one of the parenting challenges that can be identified in remarried families with stepchildren?
   a. financial strains
   b. role ambiguity
   c. negative feelings of the children
   d. interference with the parents' sexual relationship

14. _____ The text offers a number of suggestions for people who are about to enter a steprelationship. Which of the following is NOT one of these suggestions?
   a. Understand that there are bound to be periods of doubt, frustration, and resentment.
   b. Discuss the disposition of family finances with your future spouse.
   c. Examine your motives and those of your future spouse for marrying.
   d. Don't try to plan ahead.

15. _____ According to the text's discussion, consideration of various points may ease the transition process from single-parent to stepfamily status. Which of the following is NOT one of these points?
   a. Refuse to be compared with the absent partner.
   b. Understand that stepparents need support from natural parents on child-rearing issues.
   c. Acknowledge periods of cooperation among stepsiblings.
   d. Admit that you need help if you need it.

16. _____ The text points out that a stepfather can react to difficulties in finding a place in a new family in one of four ways. Which of the following is NOT one of these?
   a. He can be driven away.
   b. He may take control, establishing himself as undisputed head of the household, forcing the former single-parent family to accommodate his preferences.
   c. He can get divorced.
   d. The stepfather, his new wife, and her children can all negotiate new ways of doing things.

17. _____ Which of the following is NOT one of the stages in the seven-stage model of family development?
   a. fantasy
   b. fear
   c. action
   d. contact

18. _____ The Binuclear Family Research Project collected data from ninety-eight pairs of Wisconsin families at one, three, and five years after divorce. The text observes that at three years, remarried biological parents and their new partners had high rates of
   a. co-parenting.
   b. divorce.
   c. marital conflict.
   d. legal separation.

19. _____ What percent of divorced persons remarry within one year?
   a. 10
   b. 20
   c. 30
   d. 40

20. _____ Which of the following is NOT a reason that older couples do not remarry?
   a. children are supportive
   b. restrictive pensions
   c. Social Security
   d. feelings that it may be inappropriate

21. _____ Having children tends to _____ the chances of remarriage.
   a. slightly lower
   b. slightly raise
   c. lower
   d. greatly improve

22. _____ Which is true about remarrieds and stepchildren?
   a. the relationships between children and parents are improved
   b. remarrieds experience a difficult transition into each other's circle of friends
   c. remarrieds experience more tension and conflict than first marrieds
   d. remarrieds experience greater stability

23. _____ Andrew Cherlin referred to stepfamilies as
   a. blended families.
   b. multi-nuclear family.
   c. ambiguous institution.
   d. incomplete institution.

24. _____ A state where family members are uncertain of their perception of who is in or out of the family or who is performing what roles and tasks within the family system is the definition of
   a. a multitasking family
   b. family boundary ambiguity
   c. a nuclear-family model monopoly
   d. an incomplete institution

25. _____ Kin networks in families formed by remarriage have which of the following effects on families.
 a. new kin replace old kinship relations
 b. new kin are added to old kin
 c. new kin relationships alternate with old kin relationships
 d. new names are created for new family members

26. _____ When teen or young adult step children leave home earlier than normal for members of their cultural groups, White and Booth have called this process
 a. moving out.
 b. exclusion.
 c. family departure.
 d. extrusion.

27. _____ All of the following are steps in the process of preparing to live in a step family and create a successful family unit EXCEPT
 a. discussing modifications required.
 b. explaining the changes to children.
 c. keeping each other's children apart.
 d. giving the children an opportunity get to know their future stepparent.

28. _____ The term applied to the stepmother role based on the idea that stepmothers are cruel, selfish, and even abusive is
 a. evil stepmother.
 b. stepmonster.
 c. semistepmonster.
 d. stepmother trap.

29. _____ When the mother and her children have expectations for the stepfather and what he should do, but fail to inform him of those expectations, this is called a
 a. private communication.
 b. secret agenda.
 c. hidden agenda.
 d. exclusive agenda.

30. _____ Biological children of both partners in a step family are called all of the following EXCEPT
 a. mutual.
 b. shared.
 c. unified.
 d. joint.

Chapter 17

SHORT ANSWER

1. Summarize the history of remarriage trends in the U.S.

2. What are the differences between remarriage, in which only one person has been married before, compared to remarriages, in which both persons have been married before?

3. Ex-husbands more than ex-wives want to remarry, and do. Why?

4.   Briefly outline the remarriage advantages for women and for men.

5.   Explain what is meant by the "hidden agenda."

ESSAY

1.   Explore the extent to which remarriages are happy and stable. When they are, why are they? When they are not, why are they not?

2.   Remarried couples frequently state that it seems difficult for them to "fit in" and that they often don't know what's expected of them. According to the text, why is this?

3.   Imagine that a person you know is getting remarried and wants to know what to expect. At lunch with this friend, you explain the things you think are most important to know about remarriages. What do you tell our friend? Give a well-organized answer, taking care to be specific and complete.

4.   Explore White and Booth's study on marital quality in first marriages and remarriages.

5.   List and briefly explain each of the seven stages in Papernow's model of stepfamily development.

ANSWERS TO SAMPLE QUESTIONS

Completion

1.	Remarriages	6.	nuclear-family model monopoly
2.	Double	7.	binuclear
3.	Single	8.	Co-parenting
4.	cultural script	9.	trap
5.	incomplete institution	10.	hidden agenda

True-False (page references in parentheses)

1.	F (456)	6.	F (461)
2.	F (457)	7.	T (462)
3.	T (460)	8.	T (467)
4.	F (459)	9.	T (470)
5.	T (460)	10.	F (472)

Multiple Choice (page references in parentheses)

1.	d (456)	16.	c (474)
2.	a (456)	17.	b (478)
3.	d (457)	18.	a (478)
4.	b (459)	19.	c (458)
5.	c (458)	20.	a (460)
6.	c (461)	21.	c (461)
7.	a (461)	22.	c (462)
8.	a (458)	23.	d (465)
9.	d (462)	24.	b (466)
10.	a (462)	25.	b (467)
11.	c (465)	26.	d (471)
12.	b (464)	27.	c (472)
13.	d (465)	28.	d (473)
14.	d (472)	29.	c (474)
15.	a (472)	30.	c (475)

CHAPTER 18

AGING FAMILIES

CHAPTER SUMMARY

The number of older persons in the United States (and all other industrialized nations) is growing dramatically. Not just the *number* of elderly, but also their *proportion* of the total U.S. population is growing. Along with the impact of the baby boomers' aging and the declining proportion of children in the population, longer **life expectancy** has contributed to the aging of our population. As a group, non-Hispanic whites in the United States are older than other racial/ethnic categories.

About one-quarter of U.S. households are made up of people living alone. Due mainly to differences in life expectancy, older men are much more likely to be living with their spouse than are older women. African Americans and Hispanics are much more likely than whites to live with persons other than their spouse.

Today's older Americans live on a combination of Social Security benefits, private pensions from employers, the individual retiree's savings, and social welfare programs. Older men are considerably better off financially than are older women.

Only about 4 percent of women and of men over 65 have never married. Older married couples without children under age 18 constitute an increasing proportion of American households. Although most older people retire, some do not, and many of those who don't are employed into their seventies and eighties.

Although the majority of couples who divorce do so before their retirement years, some couples divorce in later life. Adjustment to widowhood or widowerhood is an important family transition that often must be faced by married couples in later life. Typically, widowhood and widowerhood begins with **bereavement**.

More often than spousal relationships, those between parents and their children last a lifetime. Adults' relationships with their parents can be classified as *tight-knit, sociable, obligatory, intimate but distant,* or *detached*. Research shows that there is no one typical model for parent-adult child relationships. Partly due to longer life expectancy, which creates more opportunity for the role, grandparenting (and great-grandparenting) became increasingly important to families throughout the twentieth century. Grandparenting styles vary from remote, to companionate, to involved. Effects of divorce are different for the **custodial grandparent** in comparison with the **noncustodial grandparent**.

Older Americans give to their communities and assist their adult children financially and in other ways as well. **Eldercare** (care provided to older people) involves emotional support, a variety of services, and, sometimes, financial assistance. **Gerontologists** are social scientists who study aging. The vast majority of eldercare is **informal caregiving**. Gerontologists point to two models of family caregiving: the **care provider model** and the **care manager model**. In the **eldercare team approach**, some care is personally provided by family members while other care is managed. In the **task specificity model**, family members are preferred for help. Motivated by **filial responsibility** (a child's obligation to parents) and, often, by affection, adult children care for their folks. Most caregivers are women. Many daughter-caregivers are part of the **sandwich generation**, who are simultaneously caring for their dependent children and aging parents Eldercare is a family process and involves a **caregiving trajectory**. There is considerable stress involved with eldercare. Adult children of all races and ethnicities feel responsible for their aging parents.

As America ages, providing eldercare has become a central feature of American family life. Family caregiving is important to the whole society and saves millions of dollars annually for the taxpayer. Sociologist and demographer Andrew Cherlin distinguished between the **"public"** and the **"private"** face of families.

LEARNING OBJECTIVES

Based on your careful and thorough reading of Chapter 18, you should:

1.   be familiar with the "facts" about America's aging population.

2.   understand the implications of longer life expectancy.

3.   be familiar with the racial/ethnic composition of the older American population.

4.   be familiar with the gender and the racial/ethnic differences in Older Americans' living arrangements.

5.   understand the implications of aging in today's economy.

6.   be familiar with the characteristics of marriage relationships in later life, including the postparental period and retirement.

7.   understand the implications of widowhood and widowerhood.

8.   be familiar with the relationships between older parents and adult children.

9.   be familiar with the experience of grandparenthood.

10.   be familiar with adult children as eldercare providers and gender differences in providing eldercare.

11.   understand eldercare as a family process.

12.   be familiar with racial/ethnic diversity and family eldercare.

13.   understand the relationship between the changing American family and eldercare in the future.

KEY TERMS (page references in parentheses)

acculturation (503)
active life expectancy (486)
baby boom (484)
bereavement (492)
care giver model of elder abuse and neglect (503)
caregiving (496)
caregiving trajectory (501)
custodial grandparent (495)
domestic violence model of elder abuse and neglect (503)
elder abuse(502)

elder neglect (502)
eldercare (496)
fictive kin (503)
filial responsibility (498)
gerontologist (496)
informal caregiving (496)
latent kin matrix (505)
noncustodial grandparent (496)
private face of family (505)
public face of family (506)
sandwich generation (500)

COMPLETION (using key terms)

1. The high birth rate between 1946 and 1964 created what is commonly called the _____.

2. The _____ is defined as a web of continually shifting linkages that provide the potential for activating and intensifying close kin relationships.

3. _____ refers to care provided to older people and involves emotional support, a variety of services and, sometimes, financial assistance.

4. _____ refers to the period of life free of disability in activities of daily living, after which may follow a period of being at least somewhat disabled.

5. Typically, widowhood and widowerhood begins with _____, a period of mourning, followed by gradual adjustment to the new, unmarried status and to the loss.

6. A _____ is the parent of the custodial parent.

7. A _____ is the parent of the noncustodial parent.

8. The vast majority of eldercare is _____ caregiving.

9. _____ responsibility refers to a child's obligation to parents.

10. Social scientists have noted a caregiving _____ through which the process of eldercare proceeds.

11. _____ refers to family-like relationships that are not based on blood or marriage but on close friendship ties.

12. _____ is the process whereby immigrant groups adopt the beliefs, values, and norms of their new culture and lose their traditional values and practices.

KEY THEORETICAL PERSPECTIVES

interactionist perspective
functionalist perspective (family's "public" and "private" face)

INTERNET AND INFOTRAC EXERCISES

Internet Exercises

1. Go to: http://www.babyboomers.com/. Then, click on "What Happened the Year You Were Born." Now, take a little time to explore one or more of the years encompassing the baby boom generation. If you know when your parents were born, you may wish to explore those years. After you have explored this site, respond to the following question:
    *   What kinds of events occurred during the lives of the members of the baby boom generation that help to explain the values and lifestyles of this group of people?

2.	The Social Security Administration maintains a comprehensive website. Access this site at: http://www.ssa.gov/. Once you have reached the main page, click on "Retirement." Read the contents of that page in order to familiarize yourself with the Social Security benefits that you will be entitled to as an elderly American. Respond to the following questions:
- Based upon the year of your birth, when will you be entitled to *partial* Social Security benefits? To *full* Social Security benefits?
- Do you agree or disagree that Social Security benefits should be based on how much income you have earned over your lifetime?
- Some critics have observed that without government intervention, the Social Security system may be in real trouble by 2030. Does this concern you? Are you optimistic or pessimistic about receiving Social Security benefits when you are ready to retire?

3.	As pointed out in the text, the experience of grandparenthood varies from individual to individual. For a tongue-in-cheek description of what it is like to be a first-time grandparent, go to: http://www.allaboutbaby.com/family/frstgrnd.htm. After you have read this humorous account, respond to the following questions:
- What are your impressions of grandparenthood? Assuming you are not yet a grandparent, but based upon this individual account, does this role seem attractive and one that you would like to occupy eventually in your life? Why or why not?
- The text observes that there are different styles of grandparenting. If you were (or are) a grandparent, how would you characterize your interactions – *remote, companionate,* or *involved?*

4.	Dealing with eldercare can be overwhelming. Go to http://www.aging-parents-and-elder-care.com to learn more about overcoming the challenges of care for an elderly individual. This site provides a wealth of resources ranging from finding elder care services to daily living solutions.
- What kinds of options are discussed at this site? Assuming you will at some point be responsible for an aging family member, how will you makes choices about their care?
- What are the solutions that are offered for elder care?

InfoTrac Exercises

1.	Use the keywords *the elderly*. There will be a very large number of articles to choose from. Browse through the selections and choose two or three that are particularly interesting to you. Then, prepare a synopsis of what you learned from having read these articles.

2.	Use the keyword *widowhood*. Then, focus on some key aspect of this topic, such as the economic consequence of being widowed or the psychological impact of widowhood. You can exercise considerable latitude in your selection. Read two to three of the articles that deal with the sub-area you have selected. Then respond to the following question:
- How does widowhood affect the individual survivor in reference to the sub-area you focused on?

3.	Use the keywords *elder abuse*. There will be a wide variety of articles to choose from. Select one or two that deal with "telltale signs of abuse," or "red flags to abuse." Read these articles and respond to the following questions:
- Summarize the major "signs" of elder abuse.
- What do you think can be done to combat the problem of elder abuse?

MULTIPLE CHOICE

1. _____ Terms and/or phrases like "demographic avalanche" and "age wave" refer to the
   a.   lowering of the death rate.
   b.   aging of the American population.
   c.   incidence of divorce among the elderly.
   d.   pyramidal structure of our society with regard to age.

2. _____ Between 1946 and 1964, more U.S. women married and had children than ever before. The high birth rate created what is commonly called the
   a.   birth dearth.
   b.   population explosion.
   c.   baby boom.
   d.   battle of the bulge.

3. _____ In 2002, there were _____ million women age 65 and older, compared with 14.8 million men.
   a.   20.8
   b.   19.1
   c.   18.4
   d.   17.2

4. _____ About _____ percent of U.S. households are made up of people living alone.
   a.   3
   b.   6
   c.   16
   d.   25

5. _____ In comparison with whites, African Americans and Hispanics are _____ likely to live with persons other than their spouse.
   a.   much more
   b.   equally
   c.   somewhat less
   d.   far less

6. _____ Women's Social Security benefits average about _____ percent of men's.
   a.   76
   b.   86
   c.   96
   d.   100

7. _____ About _____ percent of women and of men over 65 have never married.
   a.   14
   b.   10
   c.   8
   d.   4

8. _____ Over age 50, the quality of sex depends on
   a.   a high sex drive.
   b.   the overall quality of a relationship.
   c.   occupational status.
   d.   socioeconomic status.

9. _____   The text points out that adults' relationships with their parents can be classified in one of five ways. Which of the following is NOT one of these?
   a.   sociable
   b.   intimate but distant
   c.   economic
   d.   tight-knit

10. _____   A(n) _____ type of intergenerational relations consists of adult children being engaged with their parents based on geographical proximity, frequency of contact, emotional closeness, similarity of opinions, and providing and receiving assistance.
   a.   tight-knit
   b.   obligatory
   c.   detached
   d.   sociable

11. _____   A(n) _____ type of intergenerational relations consists of adult children being engaged with their parents on emotional closeness and similarity of opinions, but not based on geographic proximity, frequency of contact, providing assistance, and receiving assistance.
   a.   sociable
   b.   detached
   c.   obligatory
   d.   intimate but distant

12. _____   According to research conducted by Silverstein and Bengston, _____ relations between adult children and their parents are more likely to occur among lower socioeconomic groups and racial/ethnic minorities.
   a.   intimate but distant
   b.   obligatory
   c.   tight-knit
   d.   sociable

13. _____   Noncustodial grandparents are _____ to see their grandchildren as often as they had before the divorce.
   a.   equally likely
   b.   almost as likely
   c.   much more likely
   d.   significantly less likely

14. _____   A child's obligation to one's parents is called
   a.   parental responsibility.
   b.   family responsibility.
   c.   filial responsibility.
   d.   fictive responsibility.

15. _____   Social scientists who study aging are
   a.   archaeologists.
   b.   anthropologists.
   c.   gerontologists.
   d.   sociologists.

16. _____   Of the caregivers in the 1982 National Long-Term Care survey, _____ percent had been providing help for a disabled person for five years or more..
      a.   20
      b.   42
      c.   52
      d.   72

17. _____   Social scientists have noted a caregiving "_____" through which the process of eldercare proceeds.
      a.   journey
      b.   parabola
      c.   trajectory
      d.   counsel

18. _____   Jack and Janet are married with two children. They have a close friend whom their children refer to as "Uncle Harry," but this man is not really their uncle. This relationship illustrates
      a.   fictive kin.
      b.   co-parenting.
      c.   quasi-kin.
      d.   a modified extended family.

19. _____   Sociologist Arlie Hochschild has suggested that family and friends may be considered as an "informal domestic _____."
      a.   labor market
      b.   welfare system
      c.   sweat shop
      d.   social insurance program

20. _____   Sociologists and policy analysts Francesca Cancian and Stacey Oliker argue that
      a.   men ought to be encouraged to be as responsible as women for eldercare.
      b.   government-funded day care centers for the elderly are a waste of taxpayer dollars.
      c.   caregiving, both paid and unpaid, will always be viewed as unproductive work.
      d.   caregiving will always be economically costly to caregivers.

21. _____   Which of the following is NOT a strategy propose by Cancian and Oliker for more elder care outside the family?
      a.   provide government funds that support outside the family care
      b.   increase social recognition of care giving
      c.   make care giving economically rewarding
      d.   maintain an old age welfare state

22. _____   Which model of elder abuse focuses on the characteristics of the abuser?
      a.   elder abuse model
      b.   domestic violence model
      c.   culture of violence model
      d.   domestic elder violence model

23. _____   The most common form of elder abuse is
                a.   exploitation
                b.   physical abuse
                c.   neglect
                d.   sexual abuse

24. _____   All of the following are costs associated with caregiver stress EXCEPT
                a.   legal
                b.   emotional
                c.   financial
                d.   physical

25. _____   What portion of unpaid caregivers are women?
                a.   one-fourth
                b.   one-half
                c.   one-third
                d.   two-thirds

26. _____   Which grandparenting style includes grandparents doing things with their grandchildren
                but exercising little authority?
                a.   companionate
                b.   involved
                c.   remote
                d.   uninterested

27. _____   Far more widowers than widows remarry. Which of the following is an explanation for
                this?
                a.   widowers are more lonely
                b.   there are fewer available men for women
                c.   men tend to have more social support
                d.   a widower's children encourage remarriage

28. _____   The elderly population is divided into different age categories. Which is the oldest of
                those categories?
                a.   older-old
                b.   very old
                c.   old-old
                d.   senior old

29. _____   The period of life that is free of disability in activities of daily living is the
                a.   active life expectancy.
                b.   life span expectancy.
                c.   viable life expectancy.
                d.   relative life expectancy.

30. _____   The decision to retire is influenced primarily by
                a.   one's children.
                b.   one's fictive kin.
                c.   one's spouse.
                d.   one's peers.

TRUE-FALSE

1. _____ Today, children made up a smaller proportion of the population in comparison to older Americans.

2. _____ For the most part, both adult children and their parents prefer to live apart from one another, and particularly not in the same residence.

3. _____ Health costs are rising, but health insurance programs like Medicare and Medicaid are predicted to keep up.

4. _____ We tend to think of retirement as an abrupt event, but many people retire gradually by steadily reducing their work hours.

5. _____ There is some evidence that being single in old age is more detrimental, physically and emotionally, for men than for women.

6. _____ In research conducted by Silverstein and Bengston, it was observed that sons were more likely than daughters to have tight-knit relations with their mothers.

7. _____ In their research, Silverstein and Bengston found that adult children were more likely to have obligatory or detached relations with divorced or separated mothers than with married mothers.

8. _____ Declining birth rates have decreased the number of available grandchildren.

9. _____ Research shows that Americans are increasingly abandoning older people to institutional care.

10. _____ The chronically ill and disabled of all ages are increasingly cared for in hospitals.

11. _____ Asians, as well as many Hispanics, tend to emphasize the centrality of filial obligations over conjugal relationships.

12. _____ A study of older Puerto Ricans cited in the text found that filial obligation has declined in the younger generations.

13. _____ As America ages, providing eldercare has become a central feature of American family life.

14. _____ A high sense of filial obligation in a family has been positively related to actual caregiving and support.

15. _____ Unlike other Western democracies, the United States does not restrict its social insurance programs to elderly persons.

SHORT ANSWER

1.   Explain what is meant by the characterization, "America is a graying nation."

2.   Based on the text's discussion, to what extent is retirement an "abrupt transition," versus a "gradual process?"

3.   Based on the text's discussion, what are the challenges of aging in today's economy?

4.   What are the primary gender differences in the provision of eldercare?

5.   Identify and explain two racial/ethnic differences in terms of family eldercare.

ESSAY

1.   What is the *baby boom*? Who are the *baby boomers*? Why is this group of people significant in terms of aging in American society?

2.   Based on the text's discussion, explain the relationship between aging and retirement.

3.   Describe sociologists Merril Silverstein and Vern L. Bengston's typology of six indicators of relationship solidarity or connection between older parents and their adult children.

4.   Based on the text's discussion, describe the experience of grandparenthood.

5.   The text discusses a number of suggestions for better elder caregiving. List and briefly describe four of these suggestions.

ANSWERS TO SAMPLE QUESTIONS

Completion (using key terms)

1.	baby boom	7.	noncustodial grandparent
2.	latent kin matrix	8.	informal
3.	Eldercare	9.	Filial
4.	Active life expectancy	10.	trajectory
5.	bereavement	11.	Fictive kin
6.	custodial grandparent	12.	Acculturation

True-False (page references in parentheses)

1.	T (484)	9.	F (496)
2.	F (487)	10.	F (502)
3.	F (489)	11.	T (503)
4.	T (491)	12.	T (503-504)
5.	T (492)	13.	T (504)
6.	F (493)	14.	T (503-504)
7.	T (493)	15.	F (506)
8.	T (494)		

Multiple Choice (page references in parentheses)

1.	b (484)	16.	d (497)
2.	c (484)	17.	c (501)
3.	a (484)	18.	a (503)
4.	d (487)	19.	b (506)
5.	a (488)	20.	a (506)
6.	a (489)	21.	d (506)
7.	d (490)	22.	b (503)
8.	b (490)	23.	c (502)
9.	c (493)	24.	a (501)
10.	a (493)	25.	d (499)
11.	d (493)	26.	a (496)
12.	c (493)	27.	b (492)
13.	d (496)	28.	c (484)
14.	c (498)	29.	a (486)
15.	c (496)	30.	c (491)